I0823041

HOW TO DRAW A RIVER

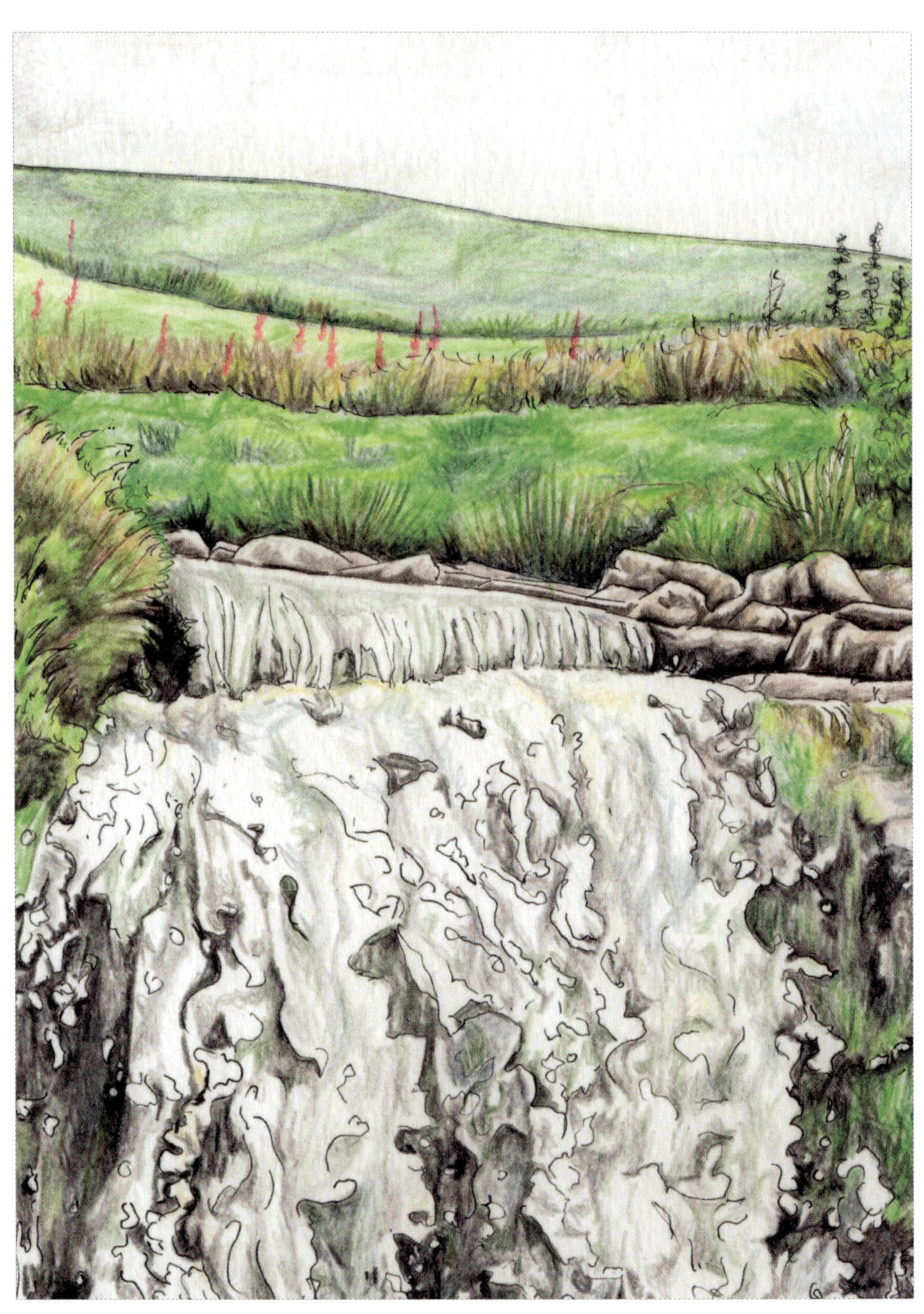

Dedicated to the memory of Joan Ives (1926–2022)

HOW TO DRAW A RIVER

From the Source to the Sea

ALEX BOON

DAVID & CHARLES
— PUBLISHING —

www.davidandcharles.com

Contents

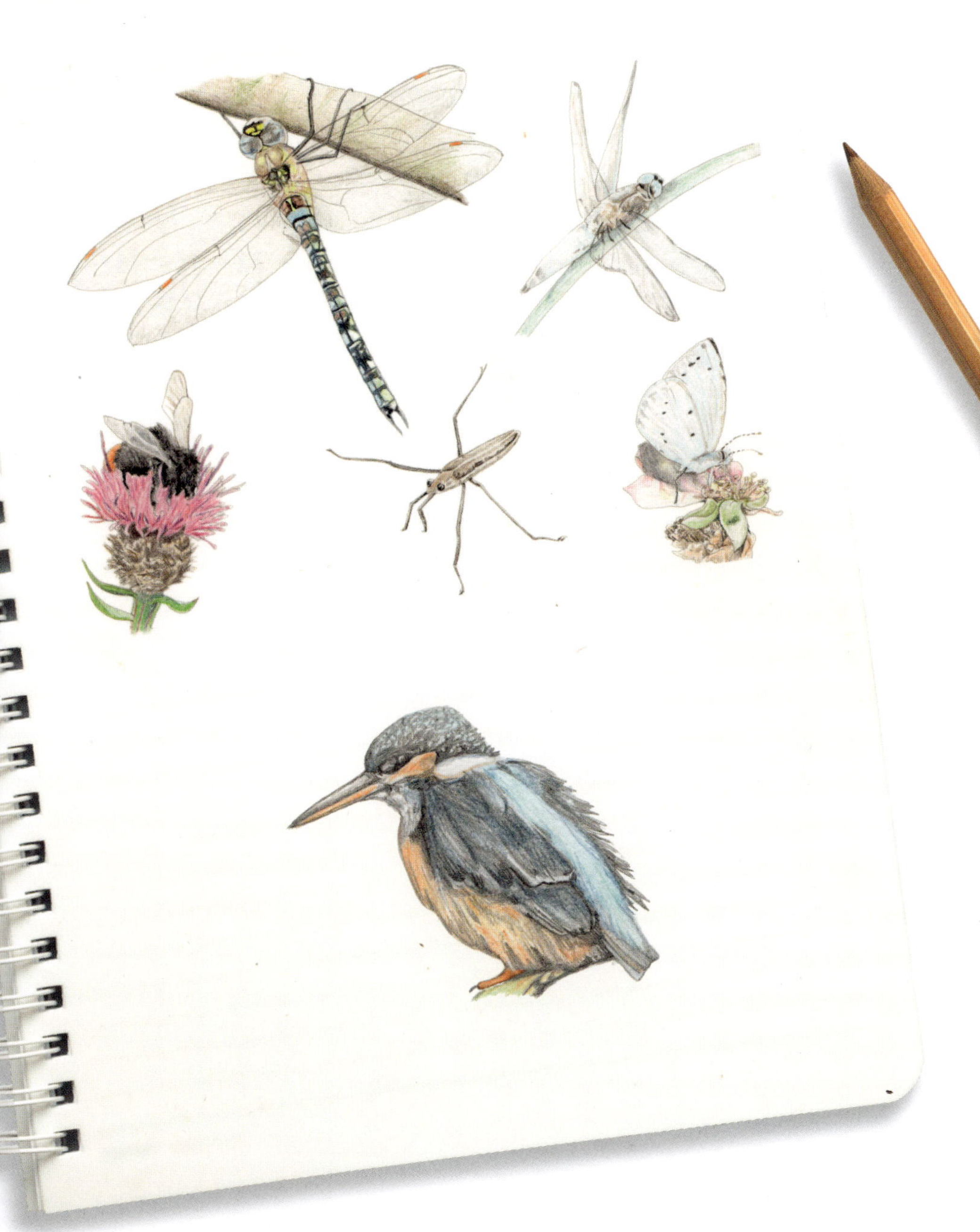

Introduction

As a nature artist, my particular passion is the continued, patient recording of a specific place and the wildlife that frequents it. Regular visits to the same place never become boring as I always discover something new, be it the flora and fauna along the riverbank, or the character of the river as it ebbs and flows. I document this in my nature journals – books that I fill with sketches and notes.

Rivers are a perfect environment for creatively recording nature. I am lucky enough to live close to a river that discharges into the sea in my home town. Documenting the seasonal changes in this river and its tributaries has brought me much joy, and getting to know the plants and birds that inhabit the river has been a wonderful learning experience. Accessing blue-green spaces is known to be great for our health and wellbeing. In addition, by getting to know our river we can recognise the signs of environmental damage and become valuable stewards of these crucial natural environments.

In this book, I hope to inspire you to get to know a river close to you. I will share a range of different methods to help you meet your river artistically and record the changes that you observe in graphite, ink, and coloured pencil. We will explore the river from source to sea, discover the wildlife that it supports, and understand how humans have interacted with it. By following the exercises, I hope that you will become more knowledgeable and enthusiastic about your local river as well as developing your artistic skills in a fun and mindful way.

Many of the exercises in this book encourage practice drawings to build an habit of observation and develop your artistic skills. Rather than finished artworks, the two images below are technical studies looking at ripples and reflection on water in coloured pencil and the use of fineliner cross-hatching to depict three-dimensional form.

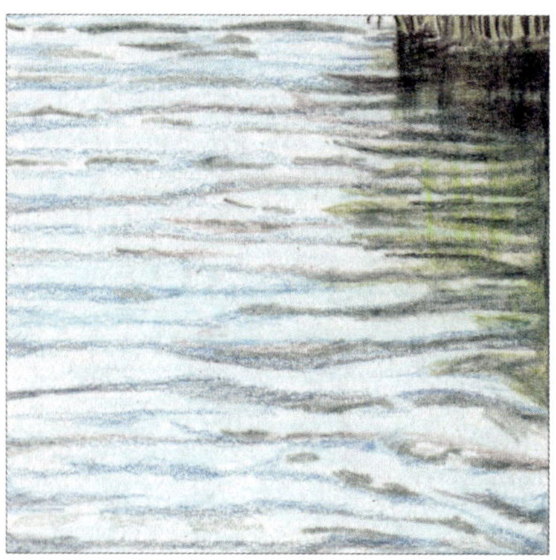

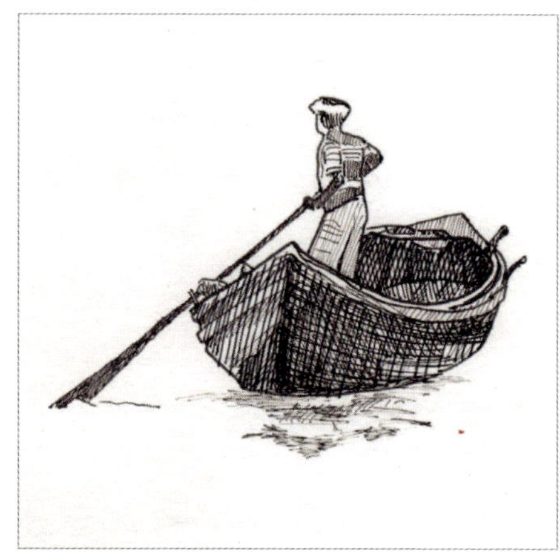

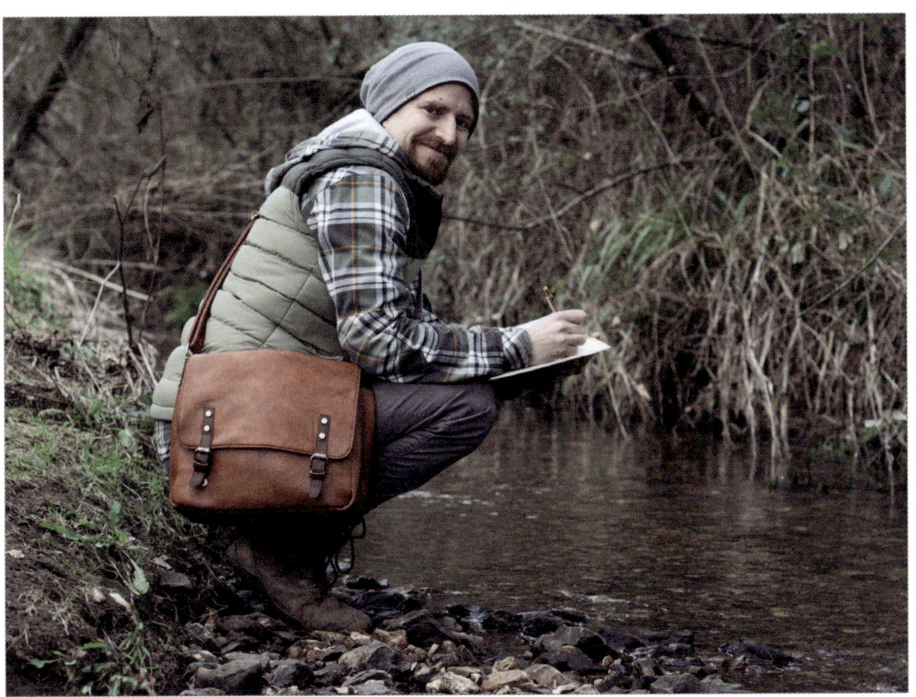

How to Use This Book

This book is divided into four chapters, each looking at different aspects of artistically representing a river. Each chapter contains four lessons using different media, usually beginning with graphite drawing, followed by linework in ink, a coloured pencil drawing, and finally something a little more adventurous. These final lessons in each chapter, and most of Chapter 4, introduce techniques such as collage and the artistic representation of data to help you explore other ways to express yourself and deepen your relationship with your chosen river subject.

The chapters take you through getting to know your river, from mastering representations of water in Chapter 1, to the specific characteristics of rivers as they move through the landscape in Chapter 2, and recording the wildlife and humans that dwell along the riverbank in Chapter 3. Finally, in Chapter 4, you are encouraged to analyse your river through mapping and data representations that draw on your creative process.

The galleries at the end of each lesson give you alternative approaches or further examples that will encourage you to expand your practice in different ways.

Getting to Know Rivers

Rivers are exciting subjects for the artist because they go through so many changes, from their beginnings as a spring or marsh to their eventual exit to the sea, a lake, or another river. No two rivers are the same and the diversity of natural life and landscape is what makes them inspiring subjects. In this book, your selected river will become your focal point for developing new artistic and observational skills.

There are as many ways to draw rivers as there are types of river! We might focus on the water itself, depicting movement in line and tone. Or we might prefer to focus on the fascinating range of birds, plants, insects, and animals present along the waterway. We might draw a series of landscapes or creatively map the river's course and how it has changed over time.

When I visit rivers, I am moved to get to know them both on the ground and through research. It is fascinating to delve into the geography and history of rivers, whether through library or internet searches or asking the locals. By keeping a river sketchbook, we can integrate ourselves with the lively world of the river, getting to know its geographical course and the people and nature that dwell in, on, and around it.

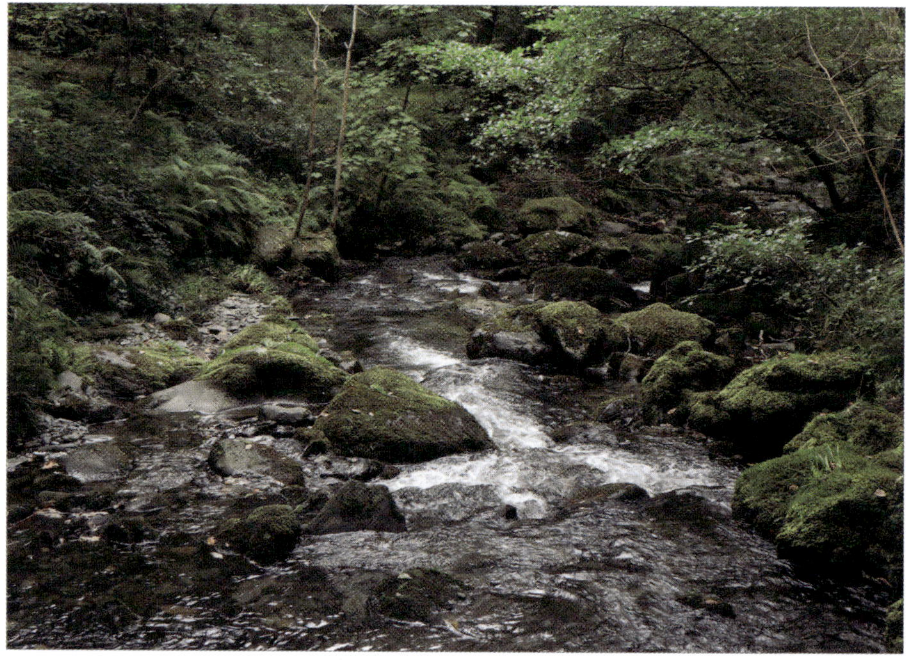

Choosing and Recording "Your" River

Wondering how to identify a river to work on for your project? Here are a few things to consider:

- **Proximity and ease of access.**
  Ideally, the river that you choose can be accessed easily at more than one point along the watercourse. Also, think about how convenient it will be to fit river visits into your life. A location that is close to something that is already routine (such as your workplace, on a regular dog walk, or near a school drop off) might help make a visit more likely.
- **A personal interest or memory.**
  Perhaps your river location means something special to you. A location along the river could remind you of someone, a special day shared with a group, or a solitary moment of nature connection.
- **Having questions.**
  Select a river that particularly inspires you to want to find out more and document it. Maybe you once saw a rare bird along its course and would like to see it again. Perhaps you know the river is in recovery from pollution and are curious about how it is recovering. Maybe there is a ruin or historic structure along the river that you have always wondered about. There is nothing like curiosity to get you fired up for a new project.

Once you have identified your river, get started with the following ideas:

- **Returning to your site as often as you can, perhaps once a week or a few times a month.**
  Try to see it in all weathers. Maybe visit your river at different times of year and at different locations along its course.
- **Taking photographs of your river on each visit as you walk the riverbank.**
  You could keep a dedicated river folder on your computer to click through and help you see the changes over time. You can either draw from these photos on screen or as print outs.
- **Keeping a sketchbook or nature journal for your on-location and at-home sketches.**
  Remember to record the date and weather conditions each time you visit.
- **Gathering materials from your site, such as fallen leaves, fronds, pebbles, or feathers.**
  Take care not to damage the riverbank or any plants when gathering and keep a close eye out for the life that calls the river home.
- **Using reference materials.**
  Learn more about the river by consulting field guides, maps, or historic photographs.

Drawing Materials

This book focuses on graphite, fineliner pens, and coloured pencils as the main drawing media. Advice about each of the main media is provided below. When other media are required, extra materials are highlighted at the start of the lesson.

Graphite Pencils

A set of good-quality graphite drawing pencils will be required. As a minimum, have H, HB, 2B, 4B, and 6B pencil hardnesses available. A good range of hardnesses will help to achieve a greater tonal range in your drawings.

Fineliners

Fineliner pens come in a range of different colours and sizes (nib thicknesses). I recommend 0.05, 0.1, 0.3, and 0.5 in black as a starting point, although thicker pens can be useful for some situations. Black ink brush tip and chisel tip pens are also useful for ink drawings. Sepia and grey fineliners are also very effective for some sketching situations. I recommend waterproof pens as standard, even if you do not intend to use paint on your drawings.

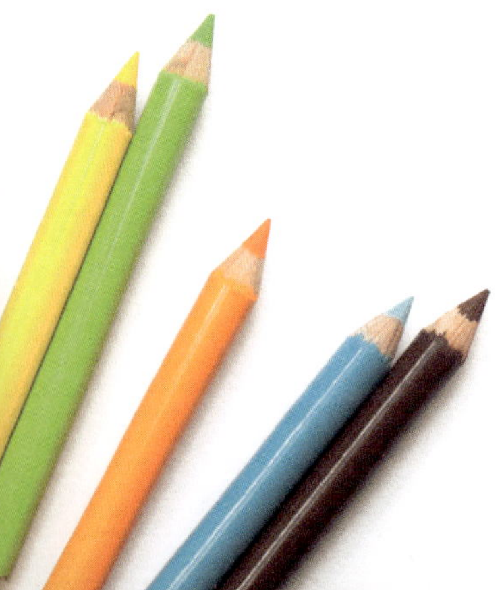

Coloured Pencils

Quality is very important with coloured pencils; buy the best you can. The best artists' coloured pencils are soft enough to blend with but hard enough to hold their form and not create dust. Good-quality, coloured pencils are also more lightfast than student-grade versions.

Paper

Choose a sketchbook of quality cartridge paper for documenting your river; an A4 (letter) size is easy to carry and large enough for adding journaling notes. However, avoid buying so nice a book that you are afraid to take it outdoors! For projects that you would like to frame or share, use a pad of hot-press (smooth) watercolour paper of at least 200gsm (80lb). Smooth paper is better than textured paper for drawing work, especially with coloured pencils as it allows them to be laid down smoothly and uniformly.

It can also be interesting to use toned or coloured papers. Toned papers provide a mid-tone from which to work both lighter and darker, and give a different feel to a drawing (see Lesson 15).

Erasers

A standard eraser is suitable for most uses; however, it may be insufficient for removing coloured pencil. I recommend a battery-operated eraser or pointed eraser pens, which allow accurate removal of pencil marks in targeted areas of a drawing. A large, soft brush is better than your hand for carefully removing rubbings.

Pencil Sharpener

A regular pencil sharpener is sufficient for graphite pencils, but coloured pencils will usually need to be taken to a much sharper point. Avoid using a knife as it damages the pencil. Instead, I suggest a desk-mounted battery or rotary pencil sharpener of the correct size for your coloured pencil set.

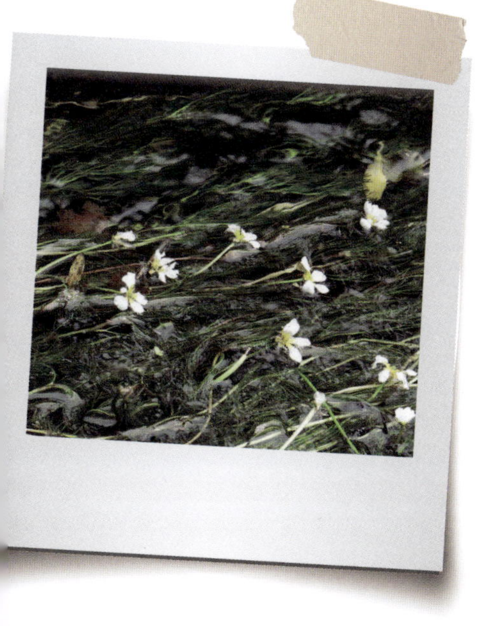

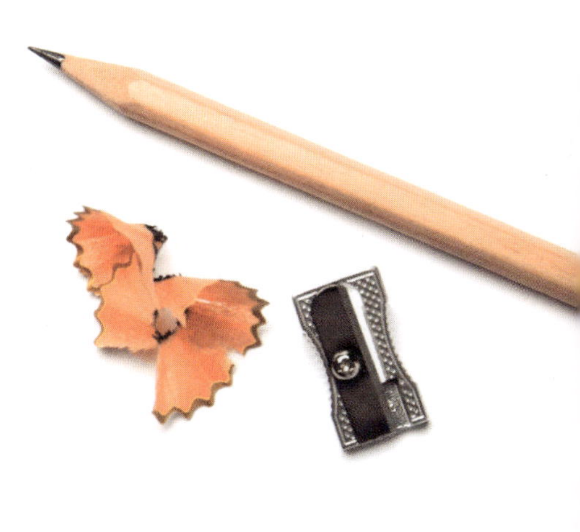

Selecting Colours

Good-quality coloured pencils are manufactured in large and sometimes continually expanding ranges of colour options. The sheer scope of available colours can be overwhelming so, to avoid investing in unwanted colours, be selective based on your intended subject.

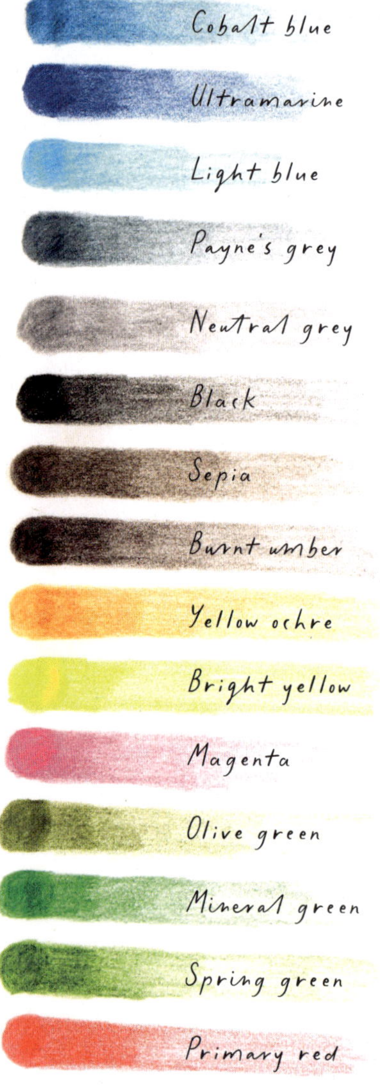

Bear in mind that the colours provided by manufacturers in smaller, pre-packaged sets are often too bright for natural subjects, so suitable colours are often best bought separately. Coloured pencils do not behave like paint – the pigments are not easily blended by a liquid carrier – so it is more difficult to blend a more subtle earthy colour from bright primaries.

As a bare minimum, I suggest the following general colours (names may vary between brands) – you can always add further colours to your set as needed:

- Light blue, bright yellow, and magenta pink
- Black, white, neutral grey, and Payne's grey
- Olive green, spring green, and mineral green
- Burnt umber, yellow ochre, and sepia
- Ultramarine, cobalt blue, and primary red

Swatch your new colours onto a sketchbook page. Press harder with your pencil on one side of your swatch and lighter on the other, so you can see the range of tones available. Label each colour so you can identify them easily.

Blending Colours

Another benefit of starting with a smaller set of appropriate colours is that you can learn to blend your coloured pencils to make satisfactory intermediate colours.

Try blending two colours together to learn how they behave. Ensure the pencils are sharp and lay the strokes down lightly using a consistent angle and back-and forth direction from one side of the box to the other. You could lay the second colour in the opposite direction to help the pigment "catch" onto the texture of the paper. The resulting colour is a combination of the two pencils. Get used to how this blending feels and the effects that you can create, as you will be using this technique throughout the lessons.

Test your ideas in squares of mixed colours, labelling the combinations so that you can call on them quickly when needed.

Try experimenting further. What happens if you reverse the colour that is laid down first? When blending, avoid putting too much pressure through the pencil. Layers need to be built slowly and gently to achieve a uniform effect.

Finally, try a simple scene, such as the river shown below. Blend several coloured pencils together and attempt to achieve a range of tones to describe the water and vegetation. Further details on using coloured pencils are given in Lesson 3.

Olive green + Burnt umber

Yellow ochre + Burnt umber

Payne's grey + Burnt umber

Light blue + Payne's grey

Payne's grey + Yellow ochre

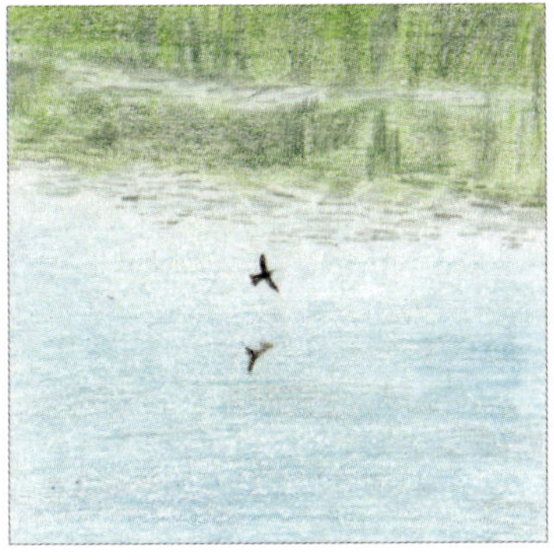

TIP:

Note that there will usually be a bias towards the colour laid on top, so it is very important to build the colours slowly with light pressure. If you press too hard right away there is limited capacity for blending.

Chapter 1

Observing Rivers

Beginning with a study of the range of lights and darks present in still water, this chapter will help you to overcome the challenges of depicting the river landscape. Once you are familiar with the effects of light and shade on a calm surface, you will tackle moving water, examining direction and flow. Quick sketches will help you to establish a coloured pencil palette, tailoring it to your river, and you will be encouraged to start recording all the life of the riverbank.

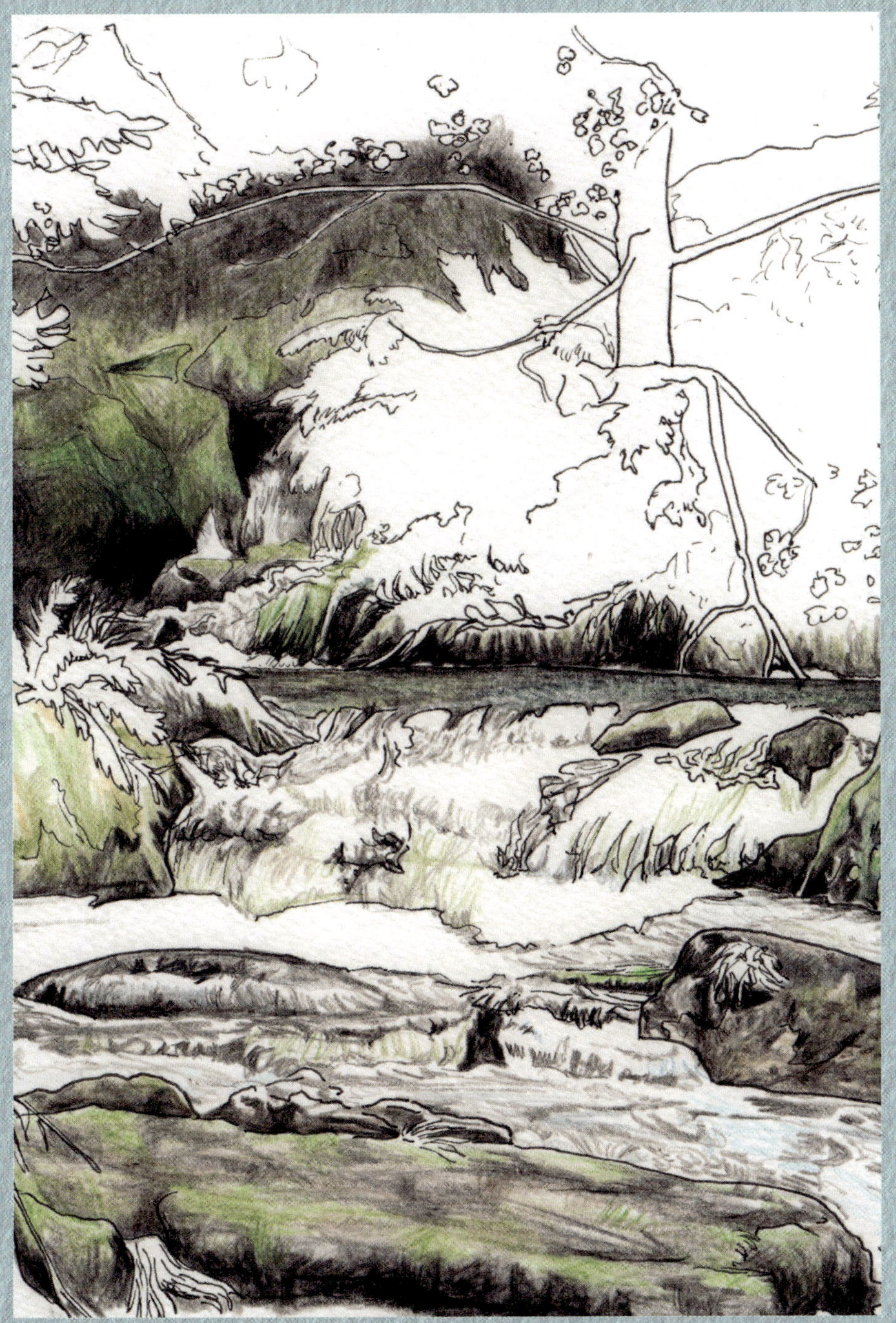

Lesson 1

Still Water

Capturing the complexity of movement and reflective qualities in water is an age-old challenge for the artist. We will begin our practice of sketching rivers by focusing on still or slowly moving water using a simple art material: graphite.

When you look at your chosen stretch of water, notice as much as you can about what gives rise to the particular tonal conditions, such as how the tonal value (how dark or light an object is) changes as the water increases in depth. Look at how the light hits the water surface, what reflections are visible and why, and how any movement in the water shows up as light and shade.

In this exercise, we will work on emulating some of the features of water using your set of graphite sketching pencils (minimum H, HB, 2B, 4B, 6B). We will explore the variety of shading that can be achieved with graphite and then advance those skills to record the complexity of still water scenes.

Warm-up Exercise: Tonal Range

Before you begin sketching, it is worthwhile practising with your pencils to see what range of tone is available. This will help you get the best contrast in your sketches later on. Don't skip this exercise; regularly exploring tone is excellent practice even for seasoned artists.

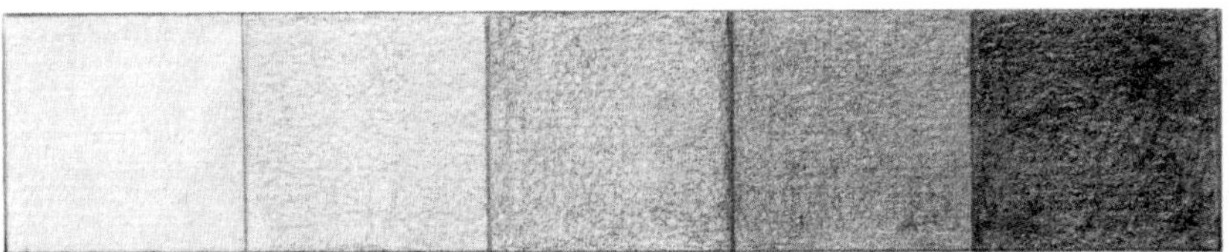

Draw five squares side-by-side in which to create a gradient. Begin with a single soft pencil (4B or 6B) and shade your boxes. Begin with the lightest possible shade that your pencil can make on one side through to the darkest possible shade on the opposite side. Work from lightest to darkest in the natural direction of your hand movement; for example, I am right-handed and moved from left (light) to right (dark).

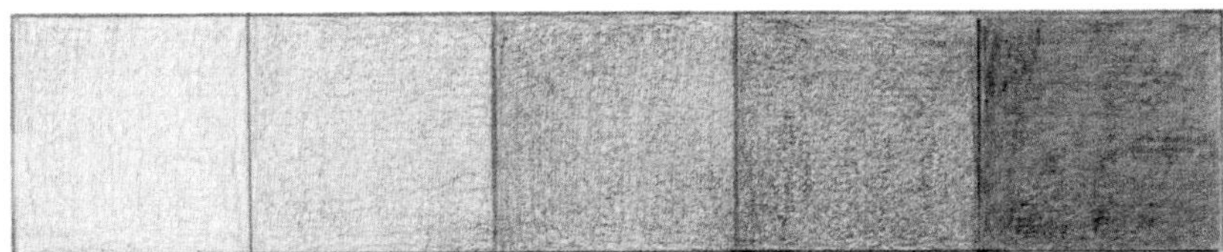

Now draw five more squares. This time, try using the range of pencil hardnesses. Use the hardest pencil (H or HB) to shade the lightest of your squares along the gradient. As you work from one side to the other, increase the softness of the pencil used. Play with what happens when you blend one pencil into another. Also notice what happens if you use a harder pencil over the top of a softer one to improve coverage. Continue to use these practice boxes to develop your skills before beginning your river drawings.

❶ Draw out some boxes on your page to contain a series of small sketches. Head out to your river location with your pencil set and sketchbook, or work from photographs. Building from the warm-up exercise, look for areas of still or slowly moving water without any bank features or obstructions and lay these down as the lightest shade. Initially, this may just be a square of a single tonal value.

❷ Features, such as the subtle ripples and the fish beneath the surface here, can be added into this single-tone square by adding another layer of pencil over the top in these subtly darker areas.

❸ Next, try an area with a bit more of a tonal range. In shallower rivers, the deeper areas may appear darker. In very deep rivers, the tone may appear more uniform. Look for where light strikes the surface, as this is the main influence on tonal value, creating contrasts along with highlights.

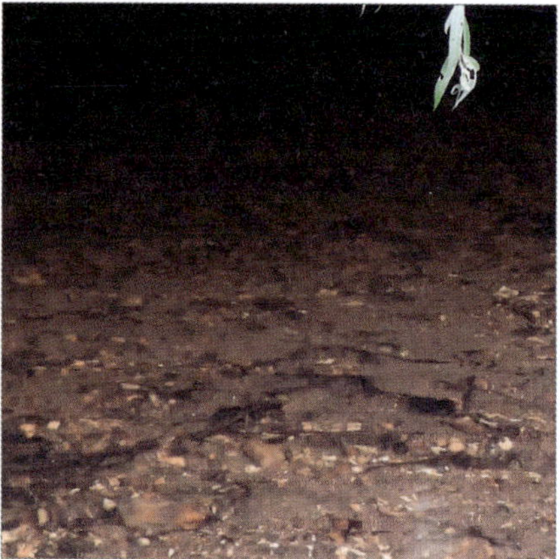

❹ Continue to gradually increase the tonal complexity by seeking out an area that has a little more movement or features below the water surface. Now you might need to use more than one pencil, applying the skills you developed during the warm-up exercise to create variety in your sketch.

❺ For your final boxes, try incorporating more of the wider river scene. In this example, I was looking at a shallow drainage channel on a marshy river floodplain. Notice that the bank features (the reeds) are drawn in more detail and with a greater tonal range than their reflections.

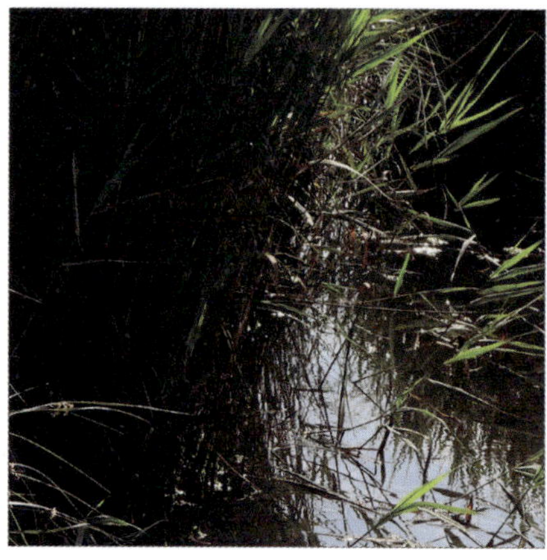

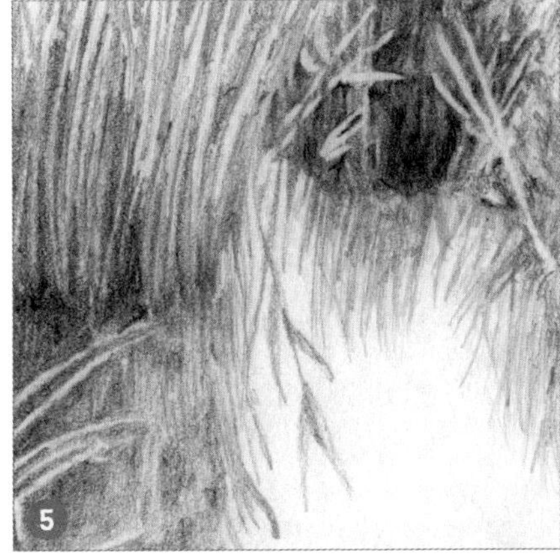
5

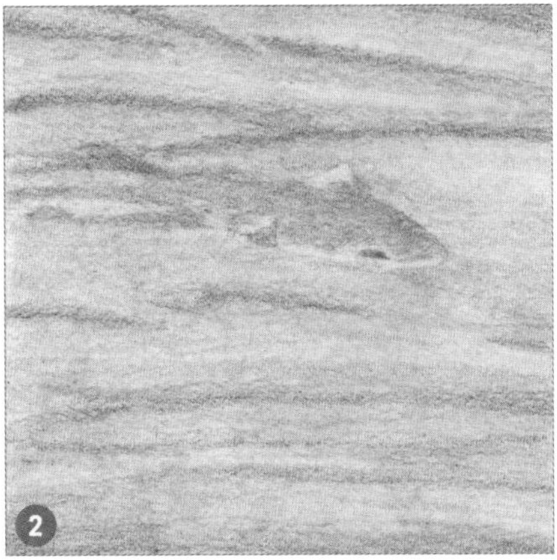

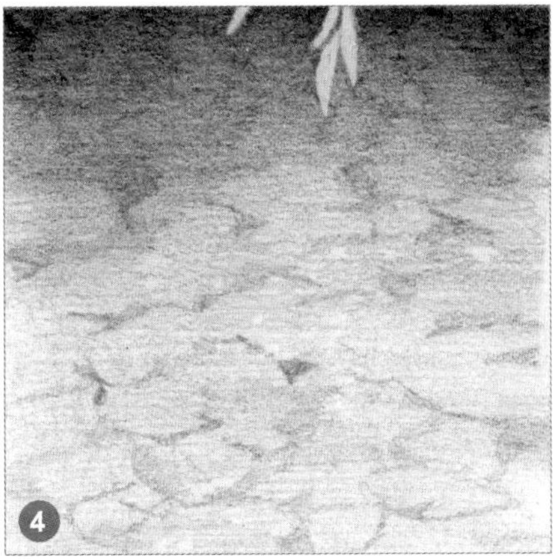

Gallery

This serene river scene uses the tonal range exercises to distinguish between bank features and the water itself. The shallow water in the foreground was left close to the white of the paper, while the complex features of the bank vegetation were given more detail. A battery-operated eraser was used to carefully bring the hanging leaves of the willow tree back to white.

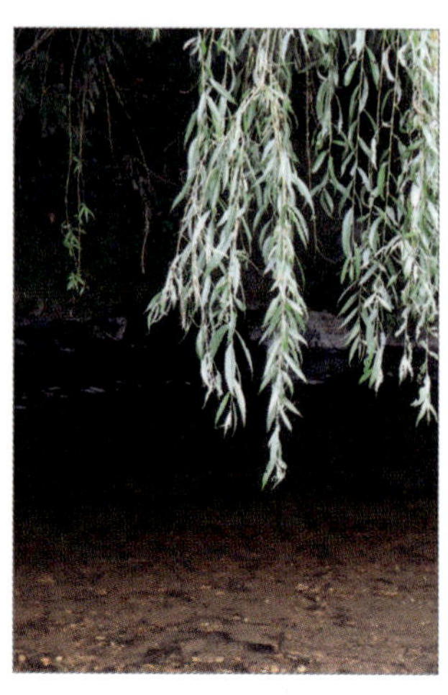

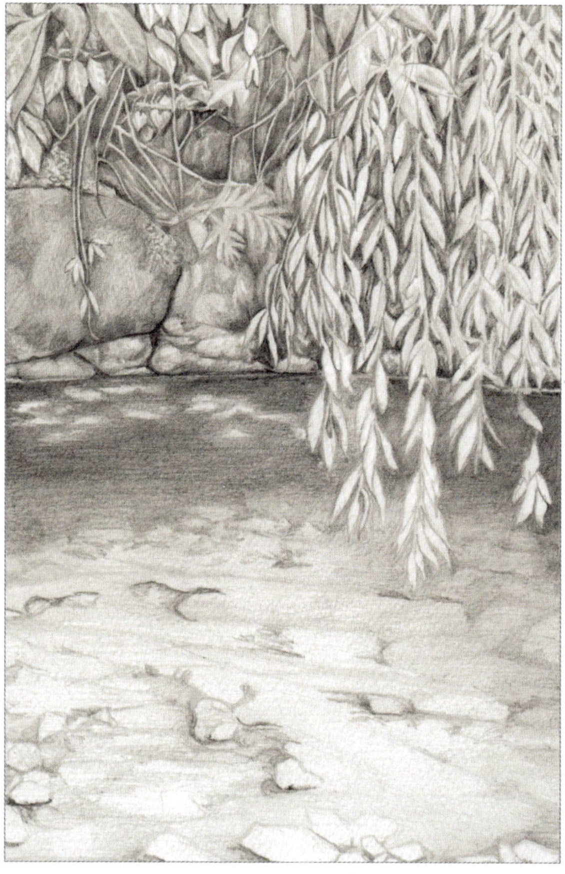

In this drawing of a more complex shallow river stream, the main distinction between the bank features and the reflections is in the strength of the shading and the level of detail. Notice the reflection is also often more indistinct than the object being reflected – in this case, the reflected telegraph wires have a clear "shimmer".

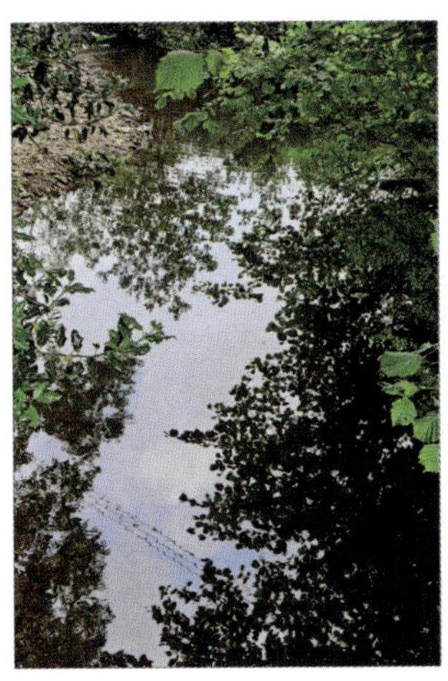

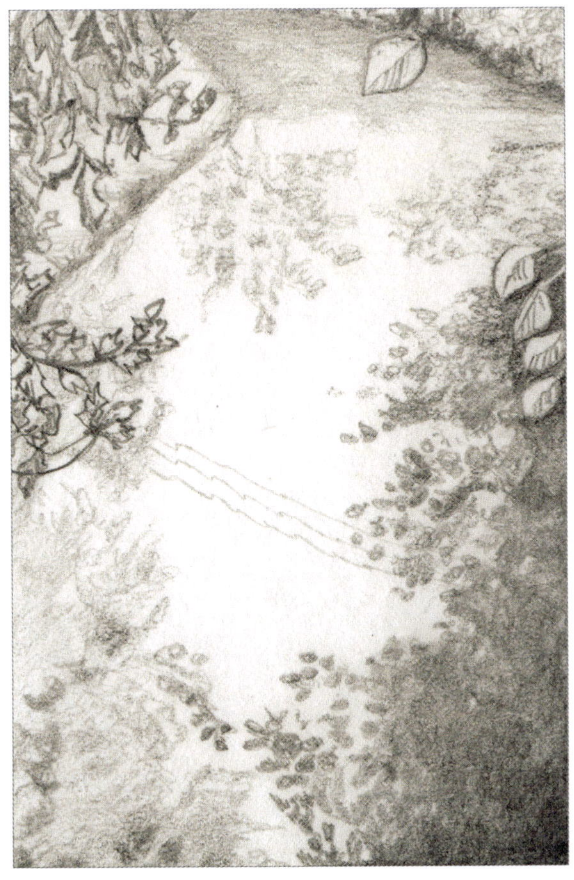

Lesson 2

Moving Water

One characteristic that every river has in common is the continuous movement of water downstream. Building on the techniques developed in Lesson 1 for pockets of still water along the river, we will now look at how to achieve a sense of movement in your river artwork.

The speed of water movement in the river will depend on several factors, including the depth and width of the stream (impact of friction), and the incline of the slope (impact of gravity). Obstructions in the water add interest and allow the flow of water to be more readily seen. Similarly, objects on the riverbank, such as tree roots and boulders, or changes in the river's course, create pockets of still water and swirling water (eddies), that can be very interesting to document artistically.

This exercise focuses on developing the skill to observe and describe moving water using lines and arrows. You could continue to use a pencil for this exercise if preferred, but I encourage the use of an ink fineliner pen. This invites immediacy and confidence in your marks as "mistakes" cannot be removed.

Drawing on Location or From Video

This exercise is best done at the riverside or from a video of moving water. Select your location with a shallow stream, or a larger river if there is a breeze or tidal flow. Avoid canals, lakes, or areas with minimal water movement for this exercise.

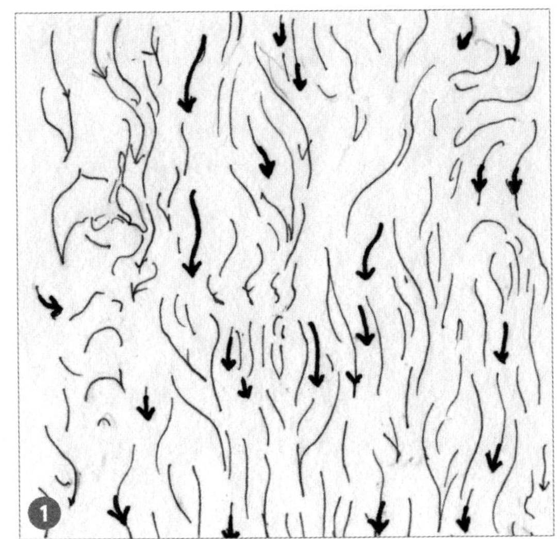

1 Choose a small patch of water. Look at the moving water for several minutes before you begin. Notice how the ripples of the water movement catch the light. Begin by trying to draw these lines of movement. Add arrows to indicate the direction of flow.

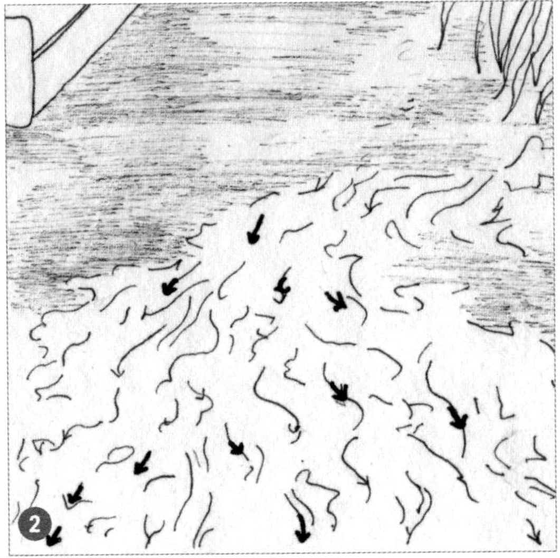

2 Next, try expanding your view. Are there areas of different water speeds or directions of flow? In my example, the river became suddenly shallower, creating a series of ripples that I described with line and arrows. Behind this, I used a similar shading technique to that described in Lesson 1, holding the pen at an acute angle to the paper to achieve the sketchy shading effect.

TIP:

Before you begin, split your page into boxes so that you don't feel you need to fill the whole sheet.

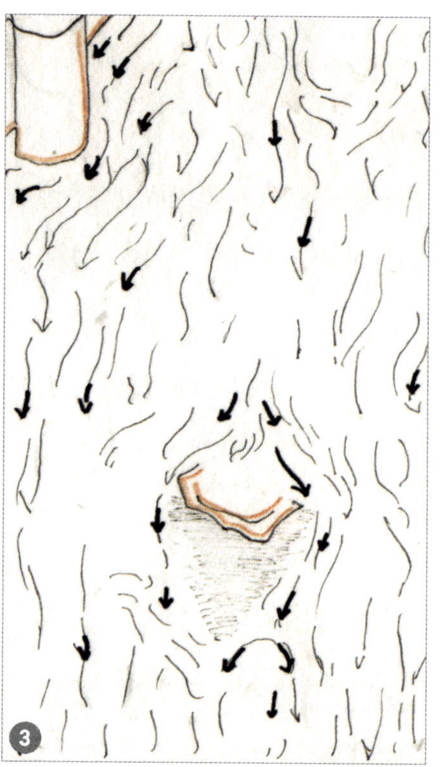

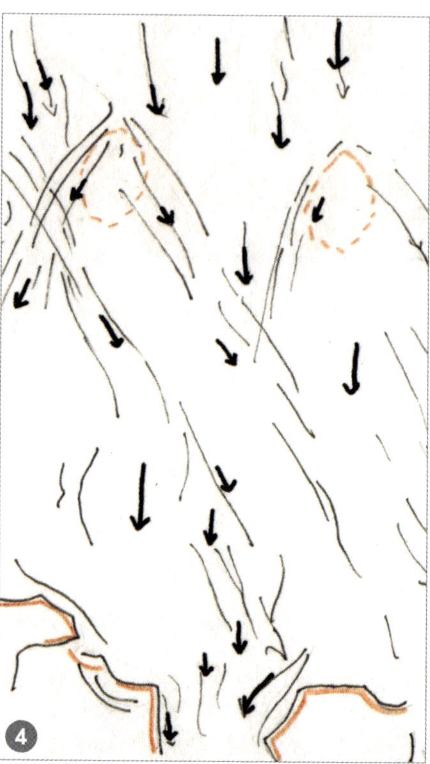

❸ Look at the river's edges and/or any obstructions to the flow. In this sketch, I noticed how the flow moved at the edge of the stream and around a rock, which emerged above the surface of the water. There was a "shadow" of still water in the lee of the rock after the flow had parted around it.

❹ Rocks and obstructions are particularly interesting when they sit just below the water, rather than emerging from it. Look for tell-tale ripples indicating the parting of the flow. Sometimes, as in this case, the ripples will overlap, creating interesting visual effects.

Drawing From a Photo

1 When working from a photo, we lose the visual information of water movement and need to make a best guess. In this example, water is flowing towards a short waterfall. There are several rocky obstacles.

2 I sketched the scene in pencil first and then used a thick fineliner pen to draw in the position of the rocks. Check the photo for indications of the flow of movement and use lines to draw the position of ripples. If you wish, add arrows to make assumptions about the direction of flow.

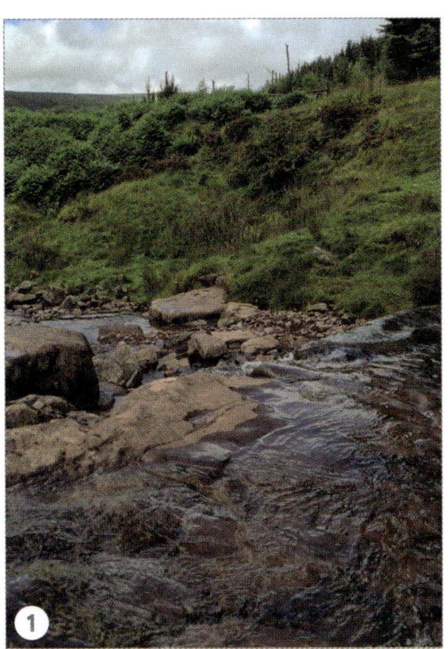

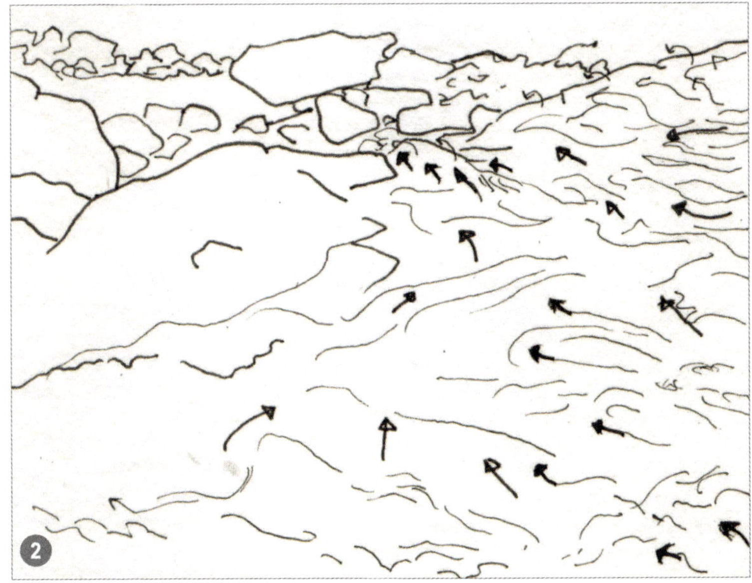

3 Waterfalls are a different case again, as photos catch just a split second of water movement. Here, we can see both the large water droplets in mid-air over the fall and the rebound of these droplets as they meet the water below, creating a foam effect.

4 Representing this in line is a challenge. As the water drops, it forms streaks and droplets, which can be sketched in using loose squiggles and expressive marks to map the white water. For a finished drawing, the addition of shading is necessary to fully bring the waterfall to life. First, try to focus on building a series of lines to create the underlying motion.

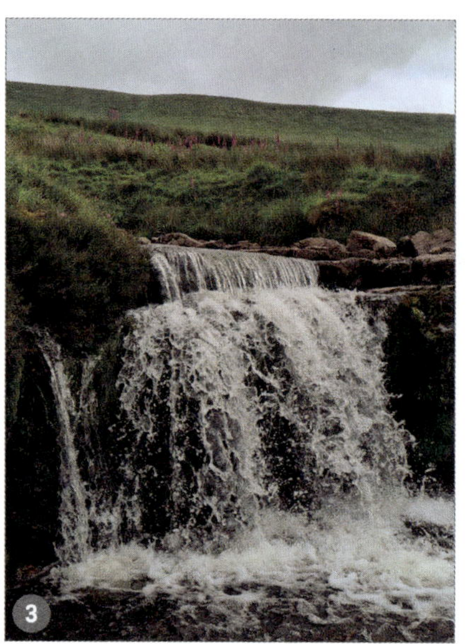

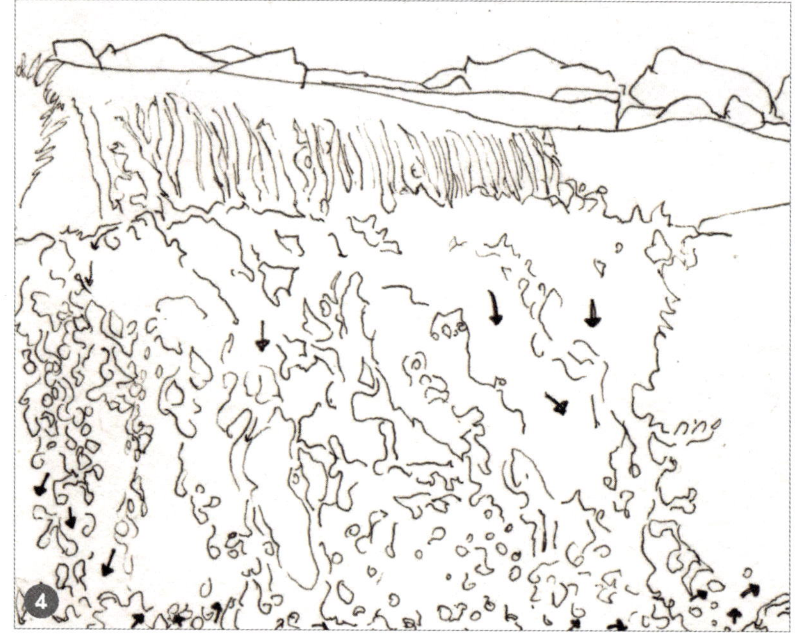

Gallery

This river scene was drawn based on the linework approach, but without the arrows! The penwork shows the difference between the still, deeper parts of the river and the rapidly moving, shallow parts. The addition of some sketchy colour finally brings the scene to life.

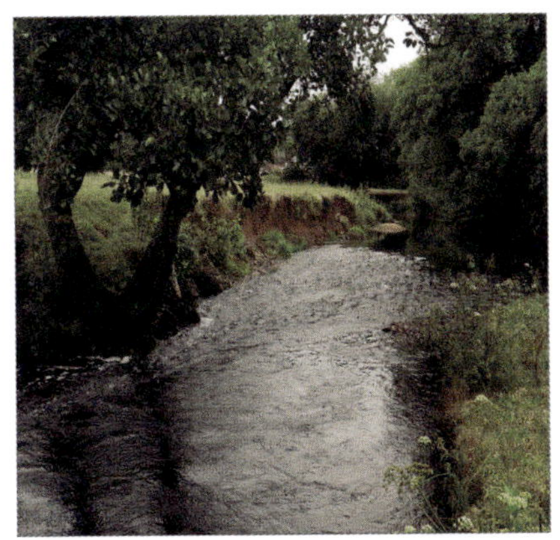

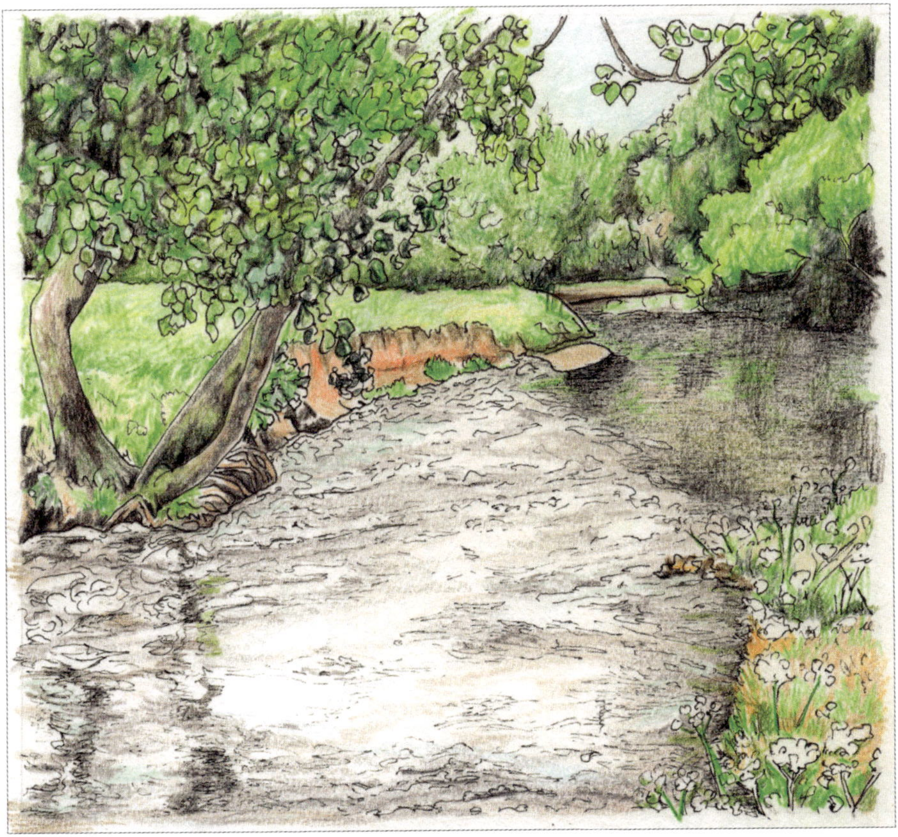

Lesson 3

River Colourscape

The colourscape of water can be much richer and more complex than it may seem at first glance. One of the most important skills for the aspiring colourist is to be able to look at a scene and quickly pick out the colours to recreate it. Being able to achieve this takes an intimate knowledge of the colours in your set and practice at blending these colours to create new ones.

When you first pick up a new set of coloured pencils, begin by swatching all of your colours on the first page of your sketchbook or a spare reference sheet of paper (see Introduction, Selecting Colours). The next stage is to see the world in the context of your set of coloured pencils. You will practice this skill in this lesson.

Developing from the graphite tonal studies in Lesson 1, you will create tonal boxes in colour based on your river. From there, you will gradually increase the complexity of the scene and the number of colours that you will need to recreate, following the techniques described in the Introduction, Blending Colours.

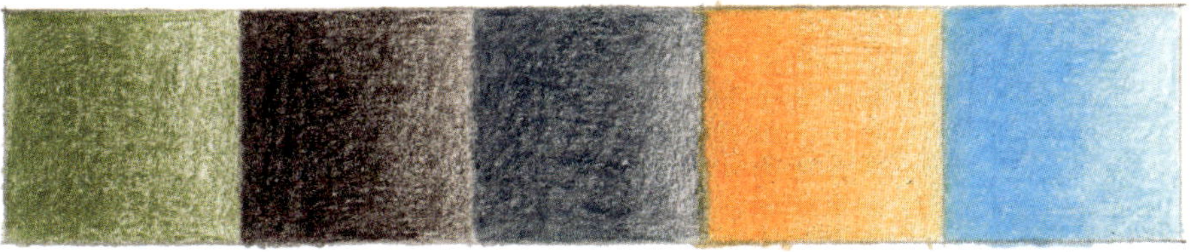

Olive green | Burnt umber | Payne's grey | Yellow ochre | Light blue

Draw five squares side-by-side to use for colour swatching. Take a look at your river spot (either on location or from a reference photo) and select five colours to form a basis for the river colourscape. If you wish, create a slight gradient in each box from the lightest to the darkest.

Box 1: A Simple Surface

❶ Head to your river with your pencil set and sketchbook, or work from photographs taken at the location. Begin with a relatively simple scene, mainly comprising water with a few riverbank elements.

❷ As for Lesson 1, draw out a few boxes on your sketchbook page to reduce the size of the area you will need to colour for each attempt. Start with a few base colours to map out the main features. Here, the dark reflections in the ripples were the primary focus of my sketch so I wanted to position these first. The inclusion of a portion of the riverbank gives some context and scale to the water drawing.

❸ With the main features in place, look for the brighter key colours in your water scene. In my river, I wanted to emphasise the green reflections of the reeds and the blue of the reflected sky on the ripples. I retained some of the white paper in the brightest areas of the reference image.

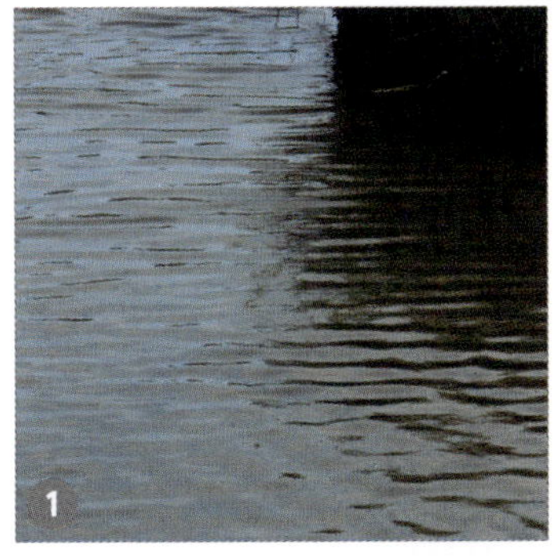

1

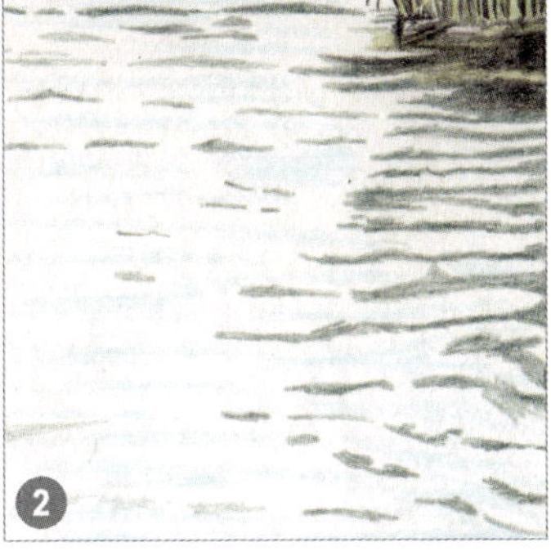

2

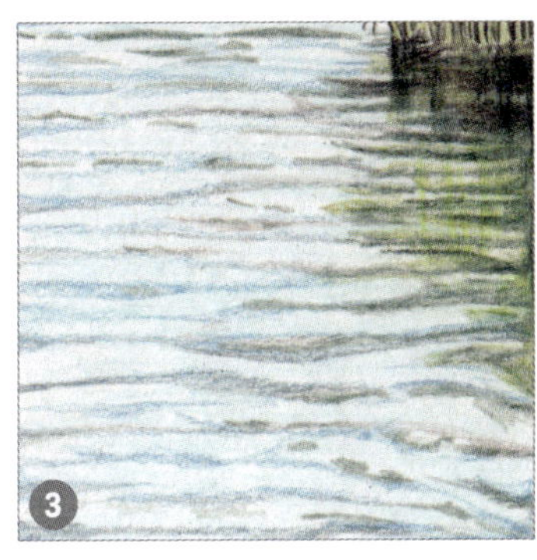

3

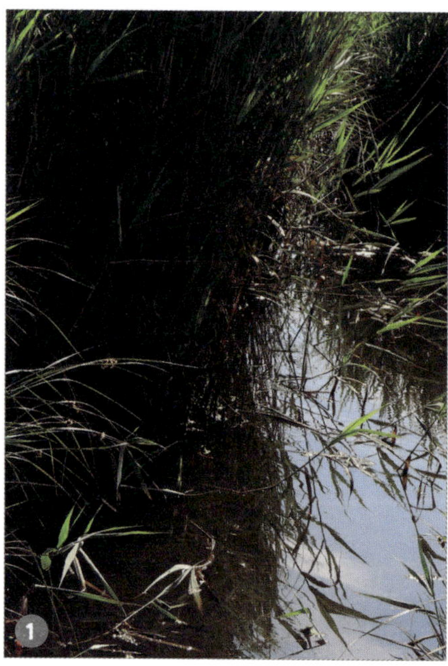

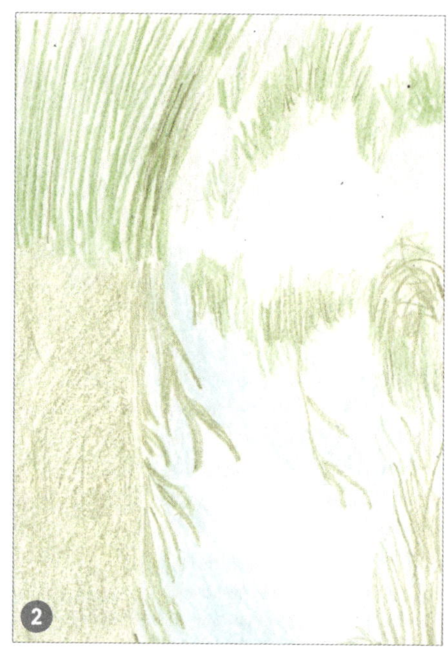

Box 2: Reflections

❶ Increase the complexity of your reference for your next sketch. Here, I have used the same image as that in Lesson 1, Step 5.

❷ This drawing is built in two main layers. Start by mapping out the areas of light and shade to position all the main elements. Here I used an olive-green pencil to lay in the main shapes.

❸ Once this underlayer is secure, the main features are laid over the top in a wider range of colours.

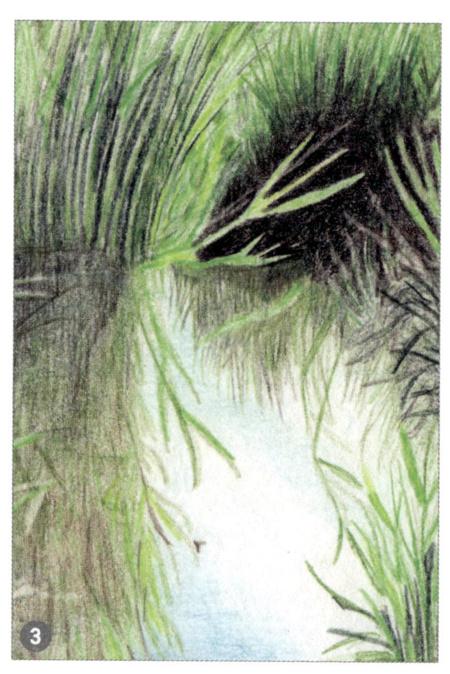

TIP:

Remember these are practice sketches. Try to avoid spending lots of time on each drawing, instead focusing on which colours you will use to rapidly recreate each scene.

Box 3: Complex Features

❶ Next, try an even more complicated scene, either incorporating more of the landscape or a faster moving, shallower section of water. Map out the key elements first; you can do a quick graphite sketch if you prefer.

❷ When sketching quickly in coloured pencil, I like to draw in the darkest areas first to immediately see where the key features of the scene will be positioned. I used a sharp burnt umber coloured pencil here, which is preferable to jet black for this stage. If you wish the area to look darker, you can add black over the top later.

❸ Continue with a limited number of colours for these quick sketches. I added three pencils (in addition to the five colours chosen for the warm-up exercise) to distinguish the vegetation and path from the water. Remember to leave areas the colour of the paper to create the effect of light.

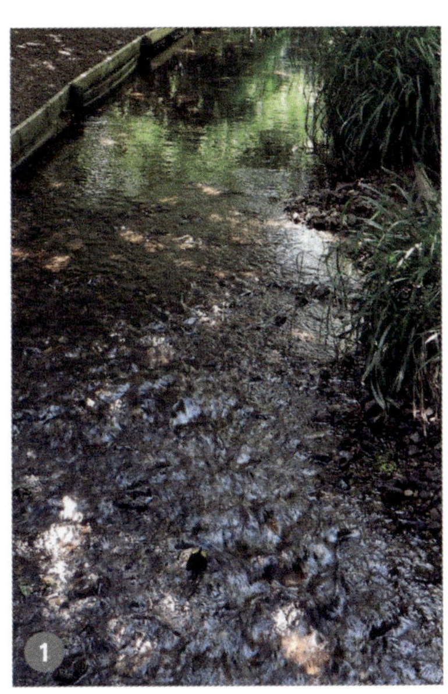
1

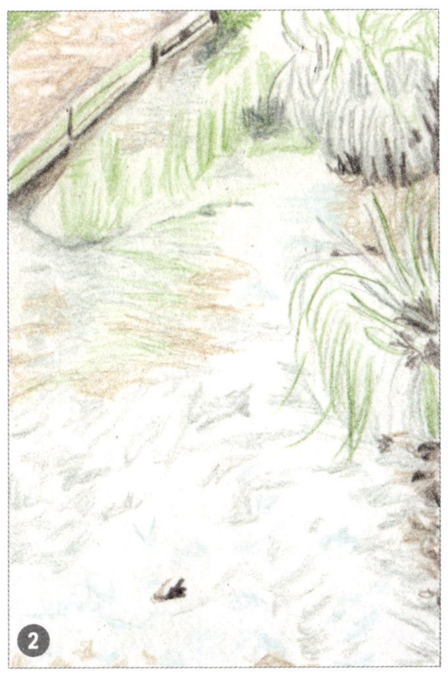
2

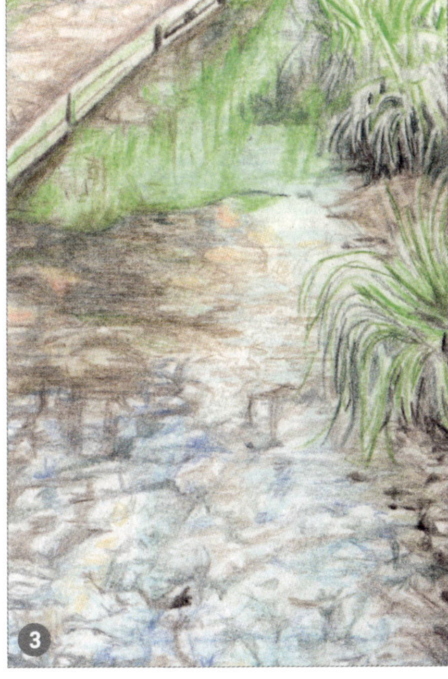
3

Gallery

Colour can make a real difference to your linework sketches. In the example below, I used the same process for the lines as shown in Lesson 2, but this time colour emphasises the shapes of the falling water. However, it is not always necessary to colour the entirety of a sketch – in fact sometimes it is better if you don't. In the example opposite, I only coloured in the river itself and the features closest to the river, bringing the attention to the water movement in a way that wouldn't be as successful if the whole image was coloured.

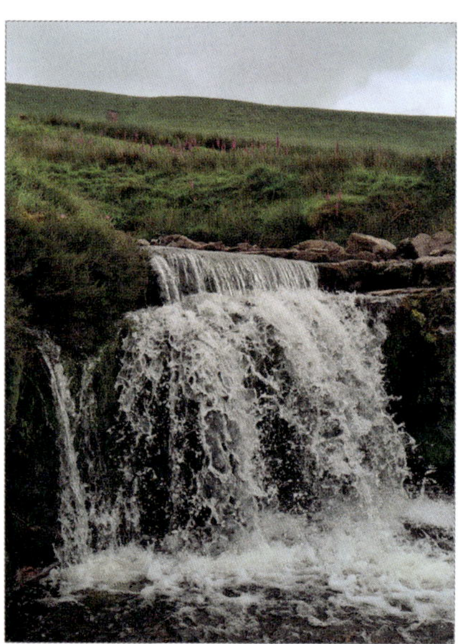

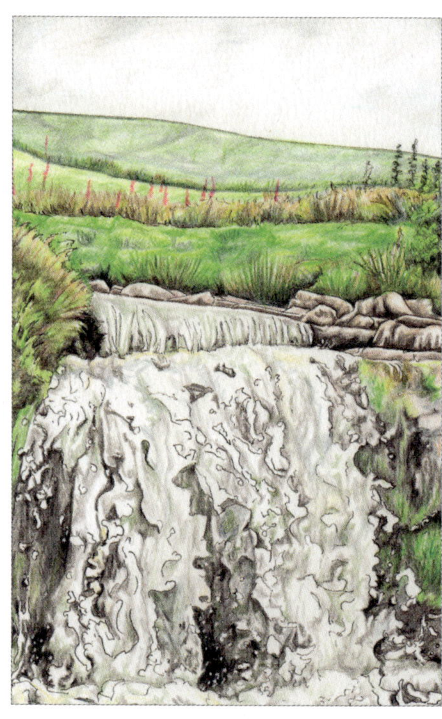

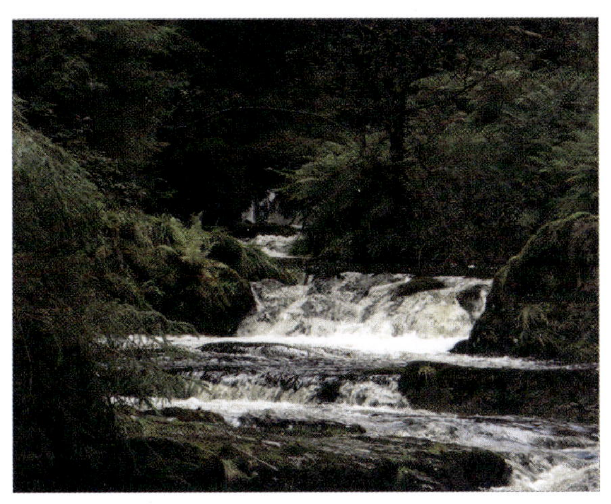

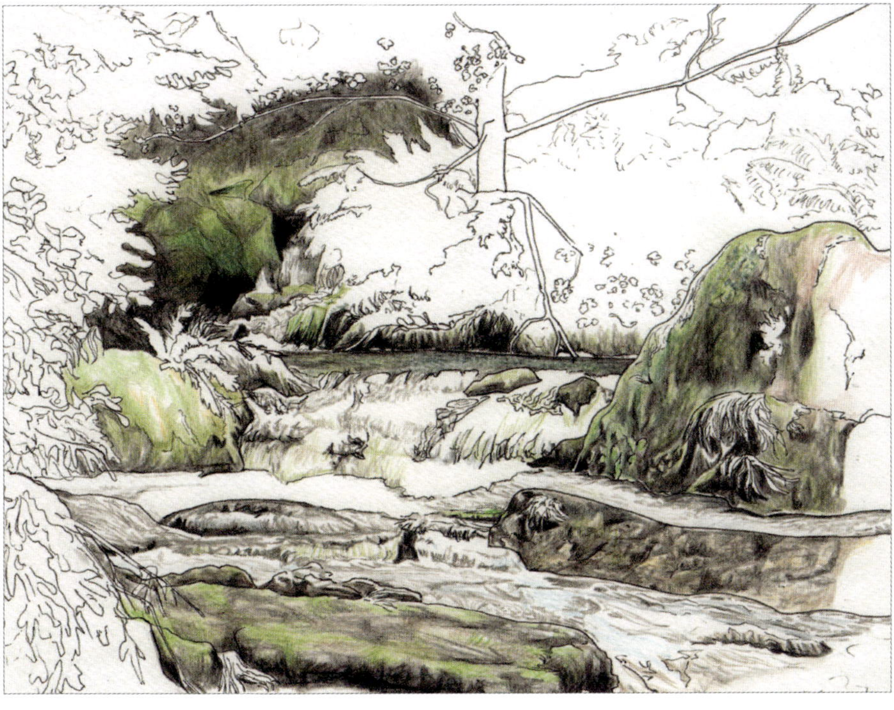

Lesson 4

A River Sketchbook

Following the lessons in this book alone will be enough to help you discover more about your chosen river. However, getting into the habit of making regular notes and sketches on location is an activity that will benefit your artistic practice for years to come. Your river sketchbook or diary might take the form of a walk log, a nature journal, or a sketchbook.

A walk log is the simplest of these ideas. Taking a page per visit, write down the route you took to reach the river and the duration of the walk in time and distance. Describe anything of interest along the river, such as wildlife or water conditions. A sketch map could be included – see Lesson 13 for more ideas.

Keeping a nature journal is an excellent way to get to know the life found along the river in an intimate way. Your nature journal will help you to creatively record your relationship with nature through words, sketches, lists, or even diagrams. Record all the life that you observe along the river and be amazed at how much more you notice every time you visit.

Visiting Your River

Nature journaling is best practised outside to unlock all the health benefits and increased observational skills. Try to make visiting the river with your sketchbook a regular habit. Even a short list or few doodle-sketches on each visit is a great starting point.

- *If possible, visit different spots along the river or walk some of the river if it is accessible. Other, more adventurous, options include canoeing or kayaking. As well as visiting several locations on the riverside, taking more time at one spot is also valuable. Perhaps bring your nature journal along to your favourite fishing or picnic spot.*
- *If you are unable to take your journal on your river visits, try to make a quick entry when you get home. Begin with just a note of the date, weather, and what you saw on the river that day. You'll be surprised at the record you can create over time from this quick diary technique.*
- *Some more nature journaling techniques to try are provided in Nature Journaling, at the back of this book.*

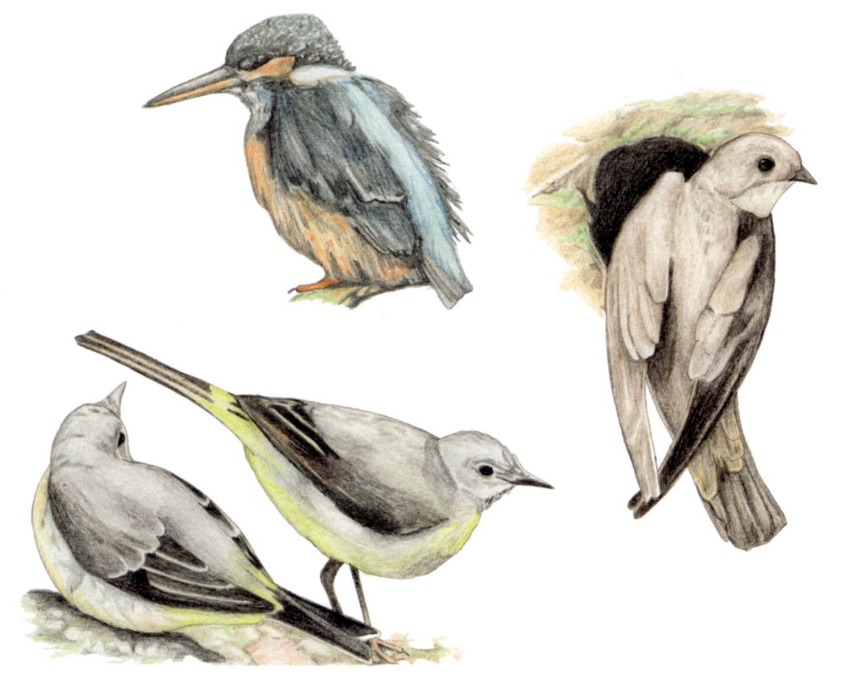

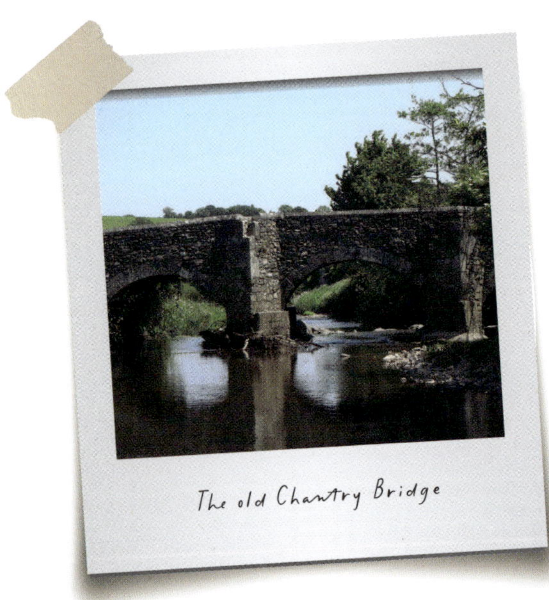

The old Chantry Bridge

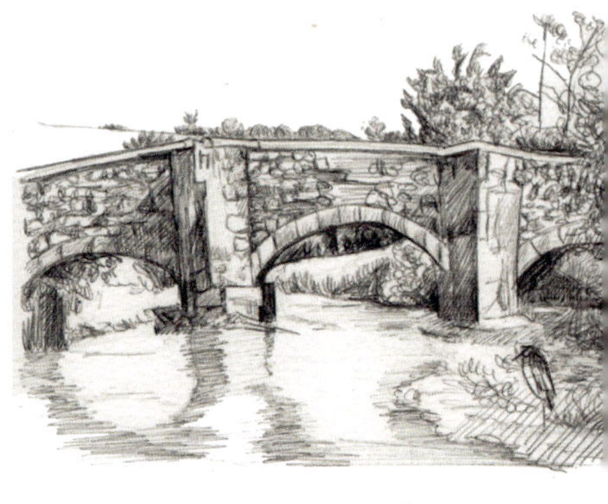

Gather supporting materials. This includes photographs, nature finds such as fallen leaves and seeds, and quick sketches in your sketchbook. You can use the photographs as reference images for drawing later. Over time you will build a repository of reference information about your river. Back at home, make sketches and more detailed drawings from some of these reference images as you fill out your river sketchbook.

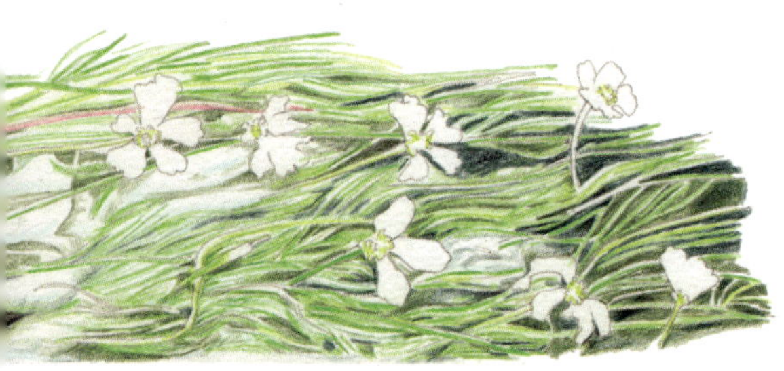

At the river, try gathering some basic data in your sketchbook. Use colour swatches to describe the clarity of the water. Decide upon a consistent reference point on the riverbank to use as a gauge of water height and describe the river level relative to that point on each visit. Some further ideas to explore river data are provided in Chapter 4.

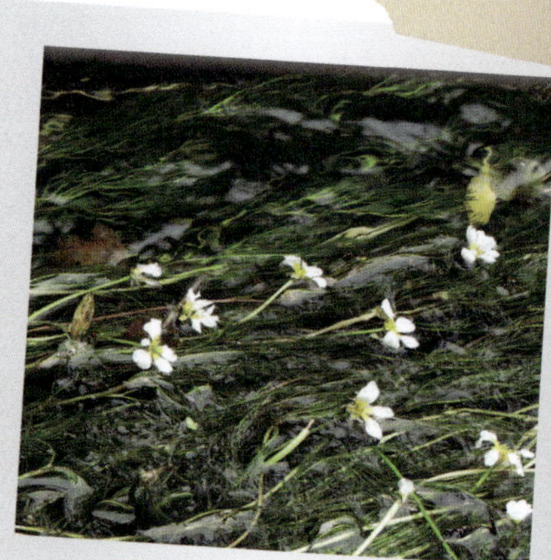

Water crowfoot
(Latin: Ranunculus aquatilis)

Brown trout (Latin: Salmo trutta)

Visit your river with your sketchbook. Record the time and date, the weather, and the conditions on the water. Write down, or sketch, anything that catches your attention or that you notice has changed since your last visit.

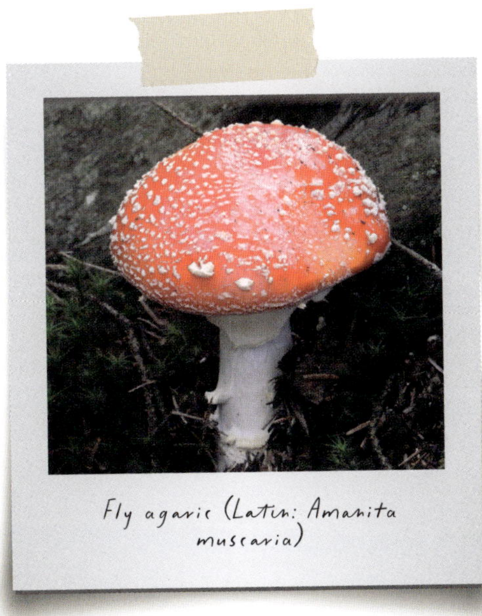

Fly agaric (Latin: Amanita muscaria)

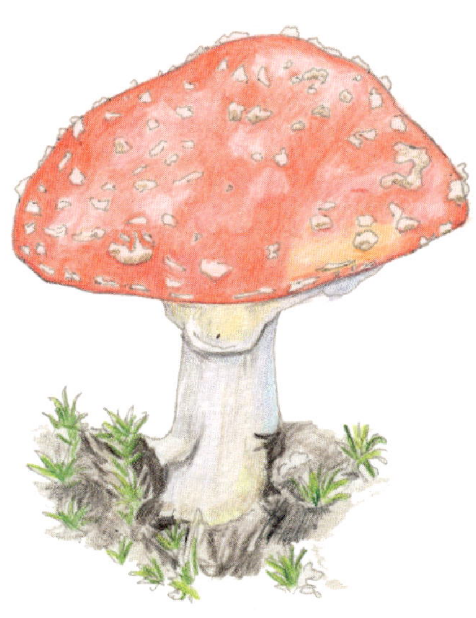

You don't need to be out by the river to make observations and gather information. The internet is full of wonderful resources such as old and modern maps, monitoring agency websites, news records, and free-to-view historic documents. If you are so inclined, make your river a research project and find out what you can. Some of this information can be incorporated into your sketchbook (see Lesson 14).

Gallery

Sometimes it is worth focusing on a specific event or experience in your nature journal. On this page, I recorded a moment I was walking along the river by the estuary and witnessed a little egret trying to chase off a very uninterested cormorant. I took a video of the event on my phone and used stills, plus a field guide, to fill in the details and recreate the action on the page.

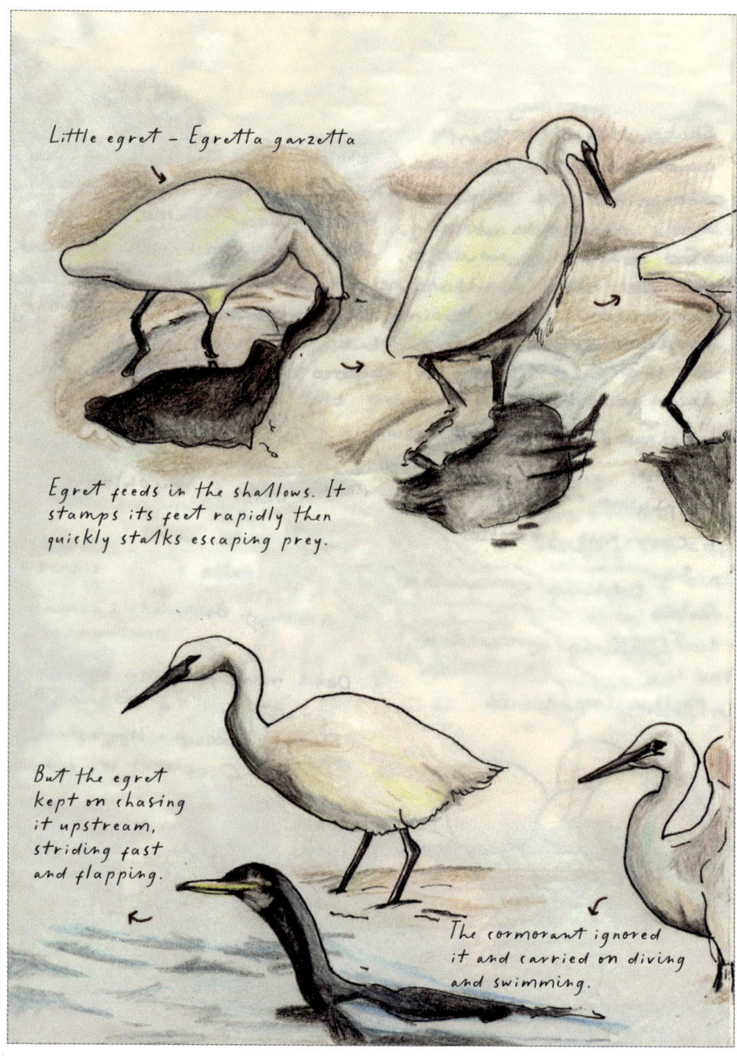

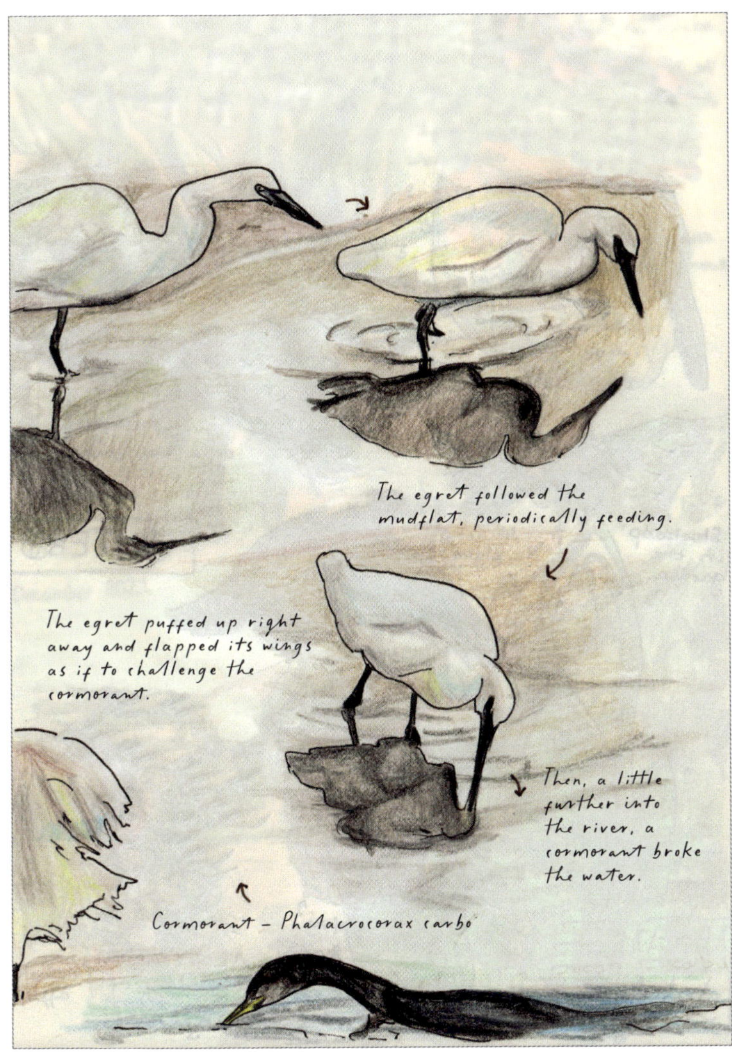
The egret followed the
mudflat, periodically feeding.
The egret puffed up right
away and flapped its wings
as if to challenge the
cormorant.
Then, a little
further into
the river, a
cormorant broke
the water.
Cormorant – Phalacrocorax carbo

Chapter 2

Rivers in the Landscape

Now that you have had some practice with the various approaches to drawing water and observing the river, it is time to start sketching different river locations. Your river's size, shape, and environment will change as it moves through the landscape from source to estuary. Studies in graphite and ink will help you to build mark-making skills to capture these changes. An exercise drawing the river in an urban setting will focus your observations on the impact of humans on the river's course.

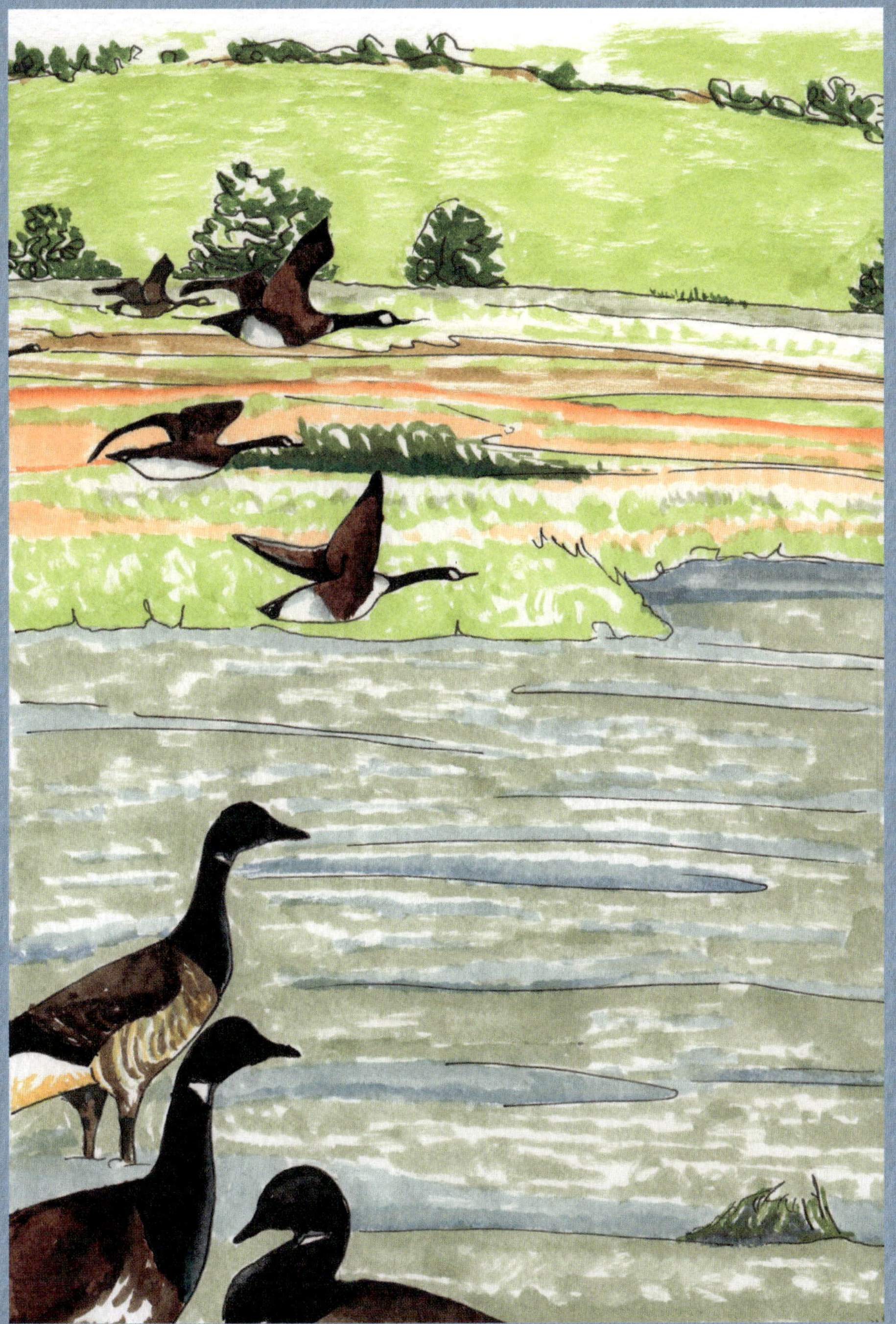

Lesson 5

A River's Source

Rivers are an integral part of the landscape, offering the artist a range of settings from which to compose an image. You may encounter mountains, marsh, floodplains, gorges, islands, and buildings along the way. With so many locations, let's begin where the river begins: at the source.

Rivers typically start somewhere elevated, such as a hillside or mountain top. They often arise from a spring (a groundwater source) but can originate from a bog or marsh, or a mountain lake. It can be difficult to pinpoint an exact source as many rivers have several, which join together in a vein-like structure as the river grows.

In this exercise, we will look at rendering the landscape of your river's source using your graphite pencil set. Note that it is important to keep your pencils sharp and have a pointed or battery-operated eraser to hand.

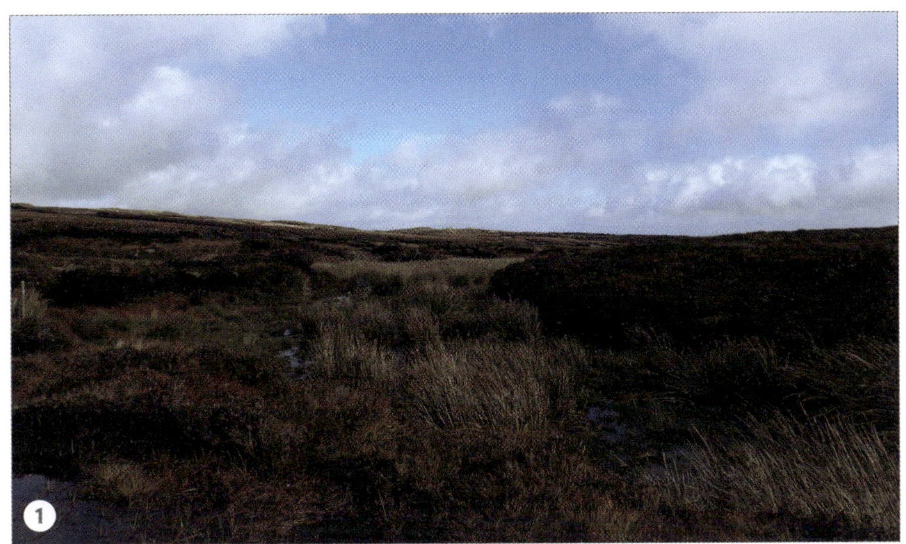

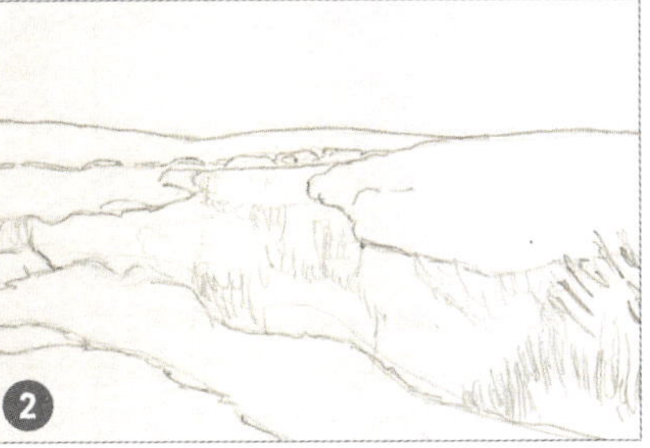

❶ Begin with a reference photo of your river's source. If it is not possible to access the source itself, consider choosing a photo of the wider landscape nearby – such as a view of the hillside, mountain, or lake where your river arises. The landscape in my reference photograph is a boggy hilltop that eventually becomes the River Severn, the longest river in the UK. You could switch your image to greyscale using a filter, or print it out in black and white, to help identify tonal variations (see Making a Greyscale Image, on the following page).

❷ Make a light graphite sketch (HB or 2B) to position the main elements. Here, I am primarily interested in the shape of the marshy river channel. Sketch out the main features that you notice. I have changed the composition of the sketch relative to the reference photo – I moved the horizon line higher to minimise the sky and ensure the focus is on the boggy foreground.

Making a Greyscale Image

When working in graphite (or any other single-colour media), it can be very helpful to transfer your image to greyscale before you start. This eliminates colour, helping you to see the tonal variations that you need to capture in your drawing. Here are a few ways to make a greyscale image:

- *Most smartphones or tablets will have a filter in the image-editing feature to transform a colour image to greyscale. Some devices have different options, such as sepia versions.*
- *On your device, try dialling up the contrast as well as adding the greyscale filter. This can help you find some tonal range if the photo was taken in the shade or on a day with poor light conditions.*
- *If you have access to a computer and printer, another option is to print the photo out in black and white. Be aware of your print quality settings on the computer; printing out in high quality is usually better for reference image purposes, but will require more ink.*

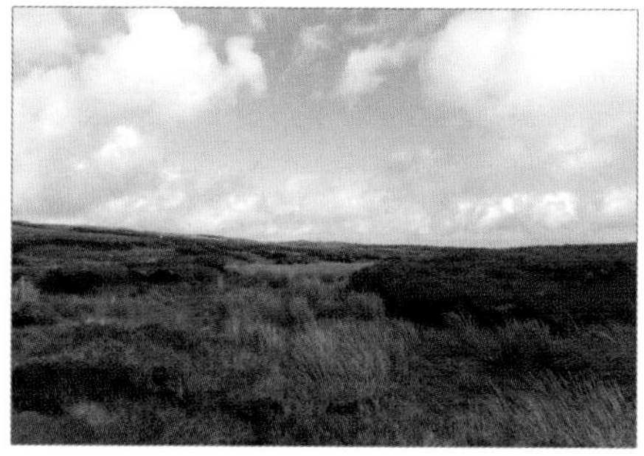

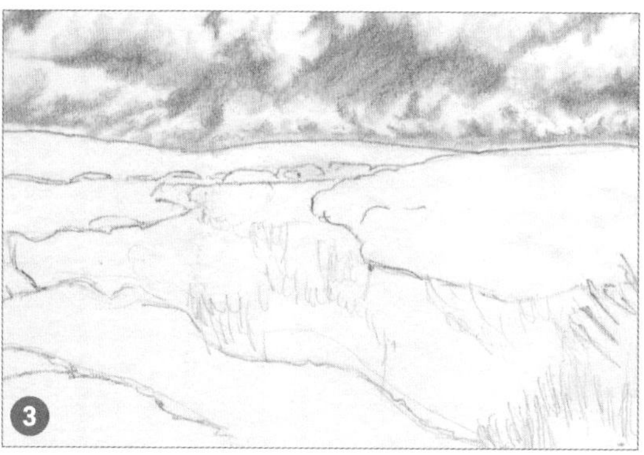

❸ Fill in the sky first. Begin in the top left (if you are right-handed) or top right (if you are left-handed) and work down and across. Use a spare sheet of paper, such as tracing paper or glassine, under your hand to avoid smudging the sketch below as you work into the picture. Use a soft pencil for the sky, smudging as necessary to soften the marks.

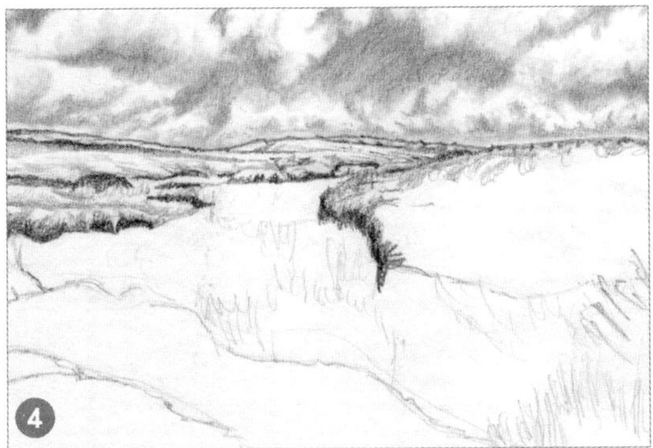

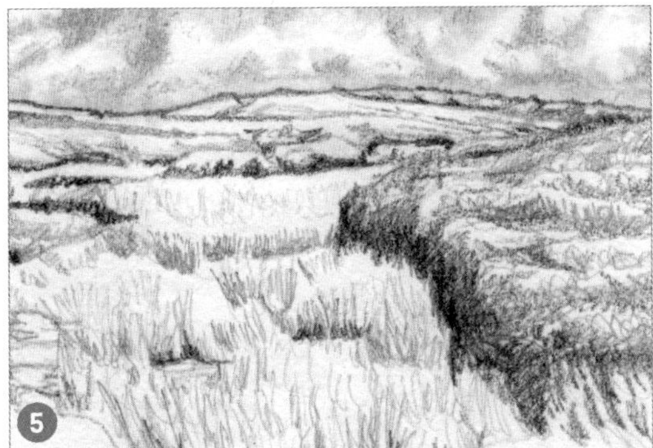

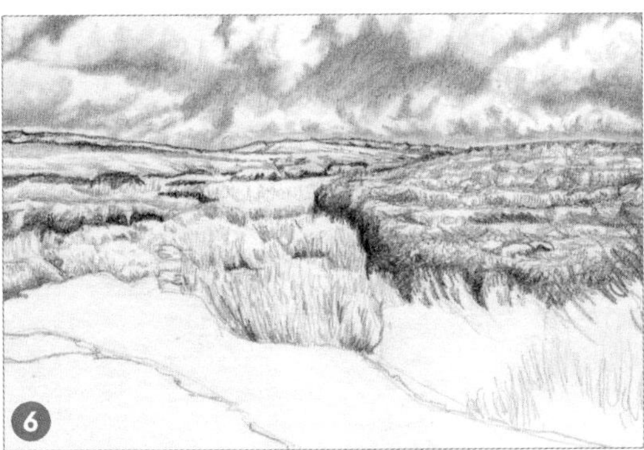

❹ Continue to work down the image once the sky is complete. I used a sharp 6B pencil to delineate the main areas of shadow. Leave lighter areas closer to the colour of the paper.

❺ Think of your previous stage as a map to which you are now adding all the detailed information. Use a hard pencil (H, HB, or 2B) to indicate vegetation, adding it in the form of squiggly marks with an appropriate leaf shape. Notice the difference in the marks between the pale reeds in the river channel and the short grasses on the banks.

❻ Work down your drawing in the direction of your hand movement. As much as possible, try to avoid returning to areas you have already drawn, instead giving each region its due attention as you work from the top to the bottom.

TIP:

Use a paper stump or blending stick rather than your finger for tidy smudging.

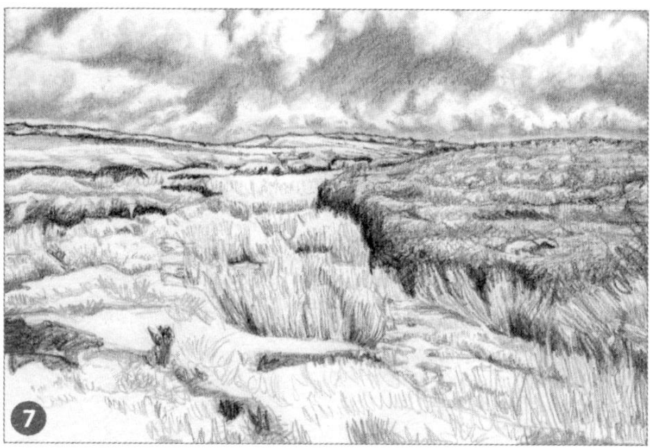

7 Look for little details to add interest. Here, I have outlined areas of water in H pencil and left them the colour of the paper to add some contrast.

8 Always look for areas that can be darkened with a strong 6B pencil and check that there are plenty of pale regions as well. It is important to emphasise, even exaggerate, these variations in tone in a graphite drawing as there is no colour to help the viewer differentiate between features. Marks can be used to express these differences as well as tone. Try to add more variety in tone and marks in objects "closer" to the viewer than those further away.

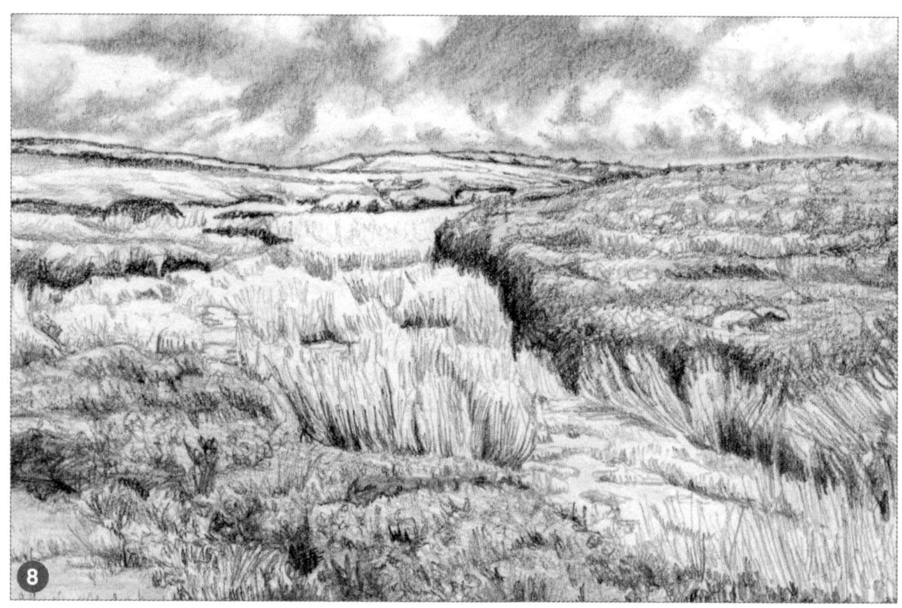

Gallery

The reference image for this mountain scene depicting a young river lacks a strong tonal contrast. It was therefore necessary to use a variety of marks to differentiate between the key features of the scene. Notice how the direction of the pencil marks is very important here, especially on the mountain slopes, helping to describe their solid form and rugged texture.

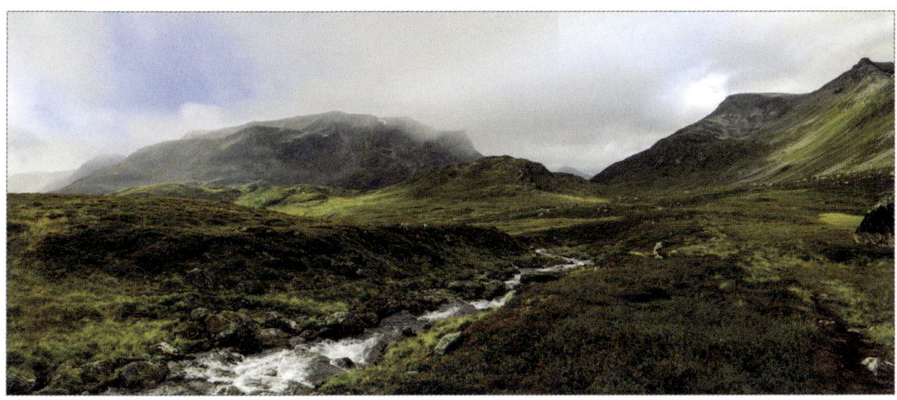

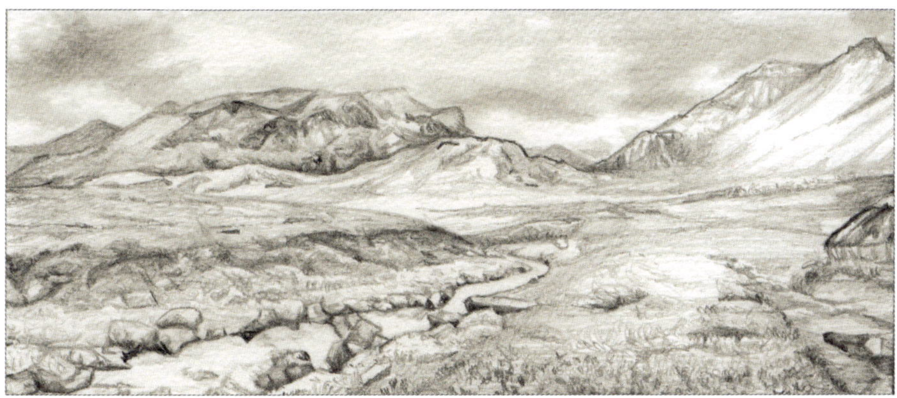

Lesson 6

A Young River

The young river is usually narrow, shallow, and fast-moving as it winds from its upland origin down to lower ground. Waterfalls are more common on the upper river stretches, and the variety of tone arising from the white-water spray lends itself to fine treatment with ink.

Sketching the young river has its challenges. Using the moving water exercises in Lesson 2 as a starting point, you will now use linework to generate contrast between areas of still and areas of fast-moving water. This will be achieved entirely through line, using differences in pen thickness, direction of pen movement, and the proximity of the drawn lines.

In this exercise, you will work into your sketch using black fineliner pens. A cross-hatching technique will be applied, giving an illustrative feel to the river drawing. Take a moment to try the cross-hatching warm-up first to get used to the technique.

Additional materials:

Black ink brush pen or ink and paintbursh (optional)

Warm-up Exercise: Cross-hatching in Ink

Before you begin your sketch, try to replicate the tonal gradient below using hatching and cross-hatching. This quick exercise will help you to get used to the action of cross-hatching so that you can apply it to different tonal areas of the river drawing.

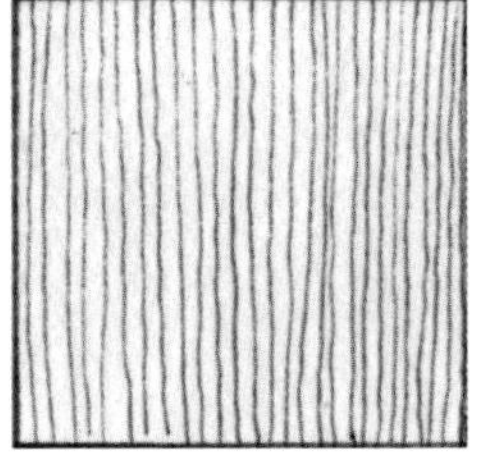

The simplest form of hatching is a series of parallel lines in a single direction. The device of spacing the lines closer together or wider apart can be used to vary the tone. Keep the line spacing as uniform as possible.

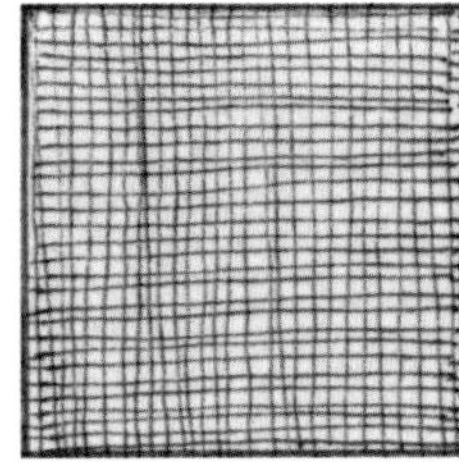

In the second box, lines have been added over the top to produce a cross-hatching effect. These lines are placed at 90 degrees over the initial lines and are a similar distance apart.

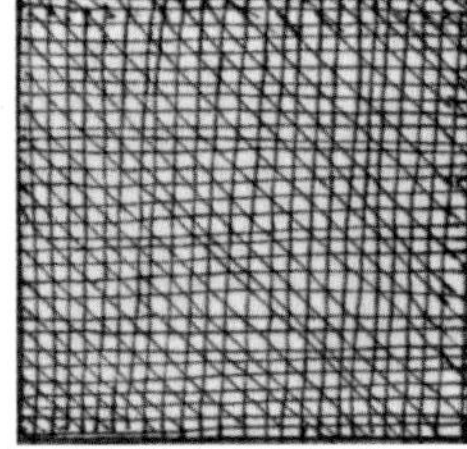

Here, a third set of lines has been added at 45 degrees to the second set, a similar distance apart. Note how the addition of these lines has further darkened the tone.

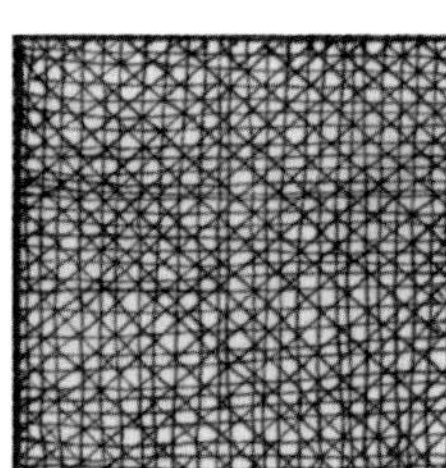

In the fourth box, a fourth set of lines has been added at 90 degrees to the third set. This gives four sets of lines at 45-degree angles to each other, like the combination of the + and × symbols. All lines are spaced a similar distance apart but, together, they build density of shading.

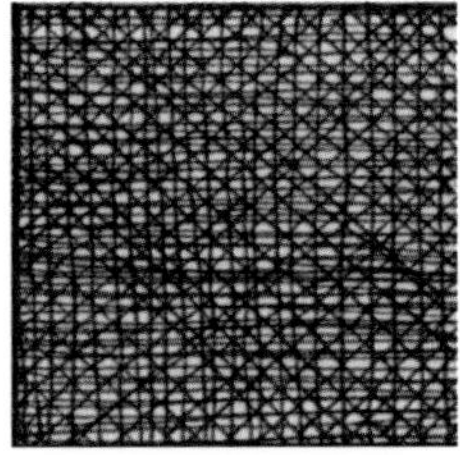

In the final box, more lines have been added in all four directions to further darken the effect. Note that only four directions continue to be used: more directions would become too chaotic, but all of the lines are now closer together.

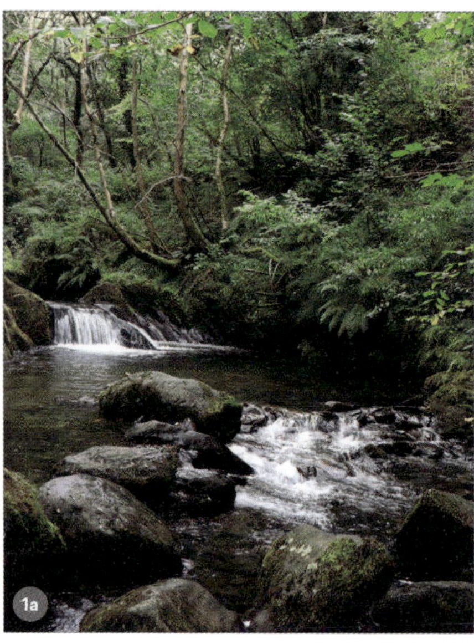
1a

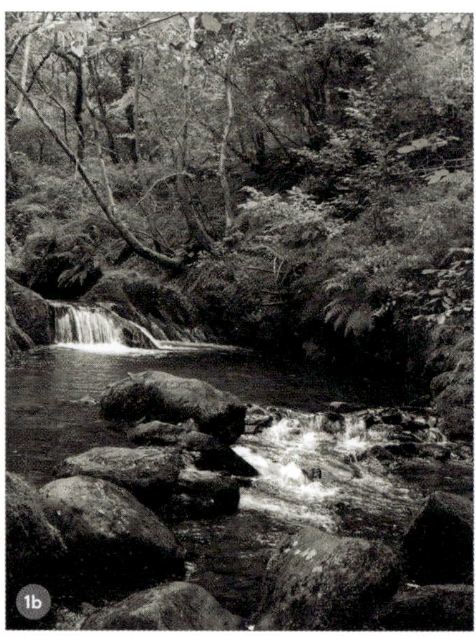
1b

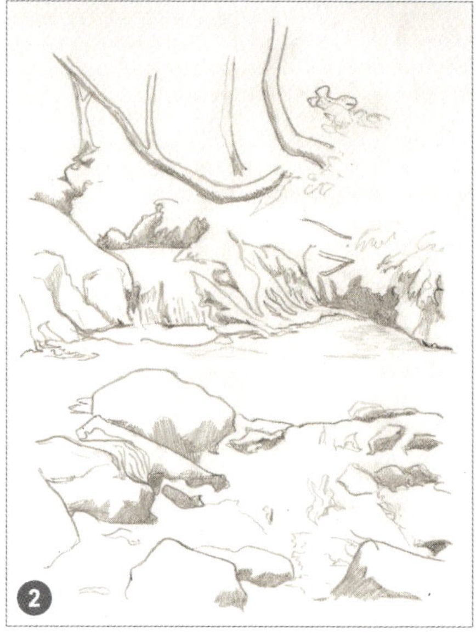
2

❶ Take a reference photo of your river in its early stages (1a). If you can't access your river, use a different image of a mountain stream or waterfall for this exercise. As for Lesson 5, you might decide to switch your photo into greyscale (1b), either using a filter or by printing it out in black and white.

❷ Prepare a quick graphite sketch in 2B pencil to position the main elements of the river scene. Pay particular attention to the positions of large rocks, trees, or other features. Shade in the darkest areas of the scene with your pencil to help with the next stage.

❸ Use a thick fineliner (size 1.0 minimum), a black ink brush pen, or some black ink and a paintbrush to cover the darkest areas indicated in Step 2 with the shaded pencil.

❹ Now use thinner pens to outline the rest of the graphite sketch. Vary the thickness of the pen according to the subject. Here, I used a size 0.3 pen to outline the rocks and tree trunks but a 0.1 pen to draw the moving water. To recreate the frothing water, I used an approach similar to that in Lesson 2 (but without the arrows!). To do this, look for darker areas within the white water in the reference photo. Outline these with the narrow fineliner pen to give an idea of chaotic water movement.

❺ Remove the pencil lines with a pointed or battery-operated eraser. Introduce your cross-hatching, starting with a thin fineliner, such as size 0.1 or 0.05. Begin with the vertical parallel lines; I positioned these on the rocks and trees. For the areas of still water, I decided to use horizontal lines. Using contrasting directions can help build the variety of mark-making needed to differentiate parts of the image.

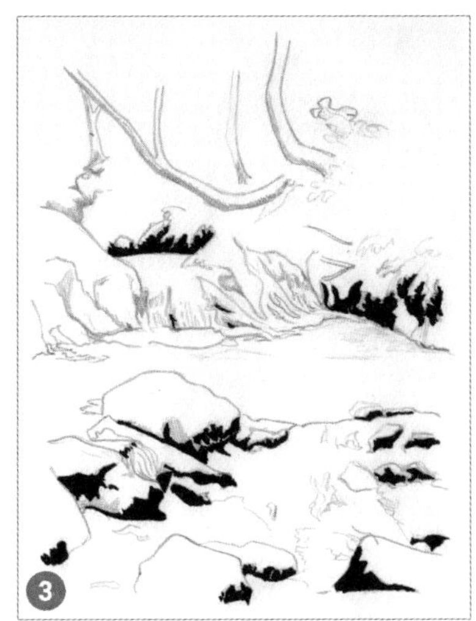

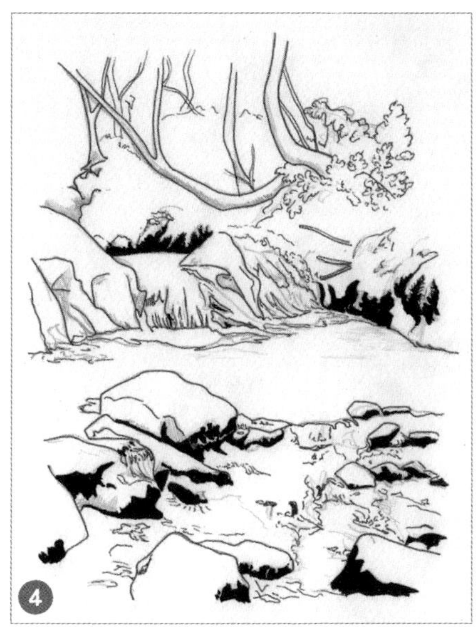

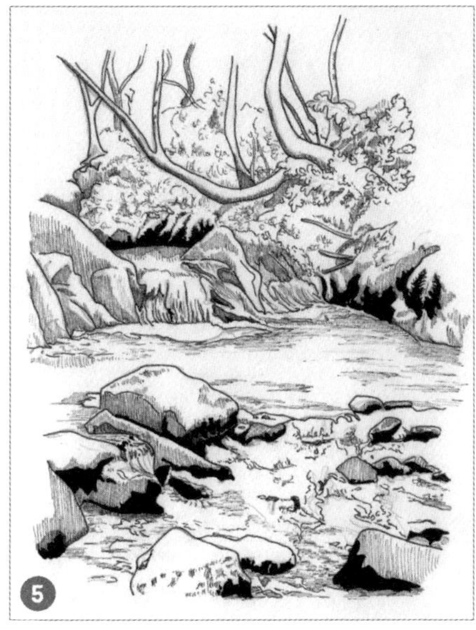

6 Work across the drawing, adding lines in the opposite direction to build up the density of tones. Some marks can be directional; for example, the lines used in the tree trunks give a sense of three-dimensionality by following the bark's texture.

7 Continue to build up the density of marks. Notice the close-together horizontal marks used for the still water and how this contrasts with the looser marks and white spaces used for the moving water, and the tight cross-hatching used for the solid shapes of the rocks.

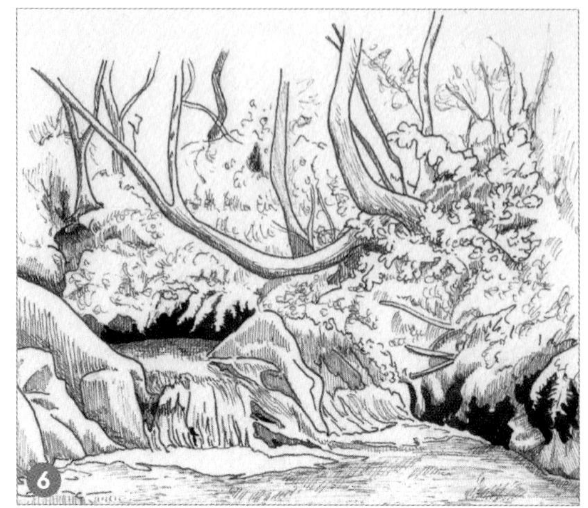

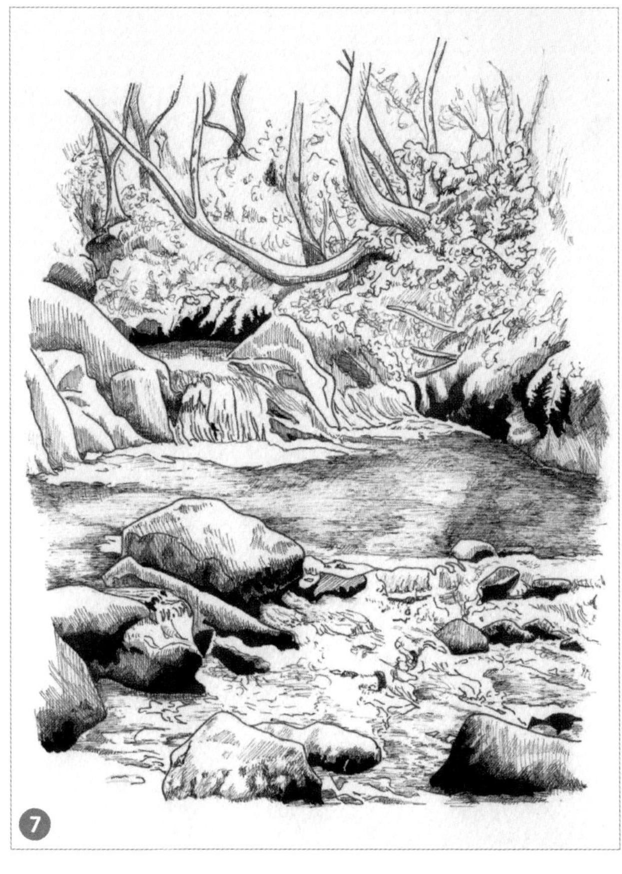

Gallery

Linework does not have to be complex. This waterfall was drawn quite simply with long, smooth lines interspersed with short curves to indicate movement. These short lines are positioned in areas of dark tone that appear in the moving white water. Rather than cross-hatching, ink brush pens were used to add some colour to the image and highlight the white water of the waterfall.

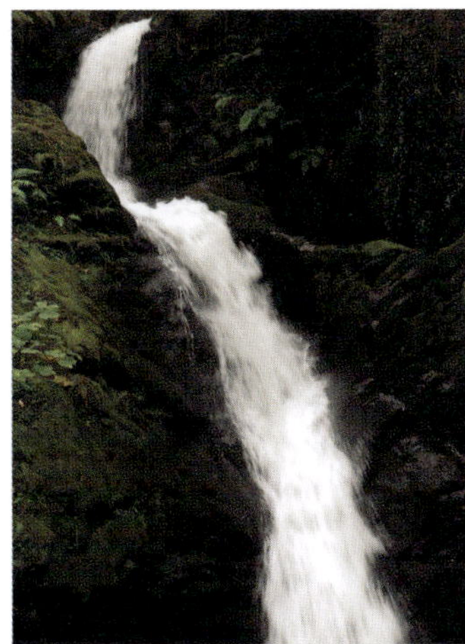

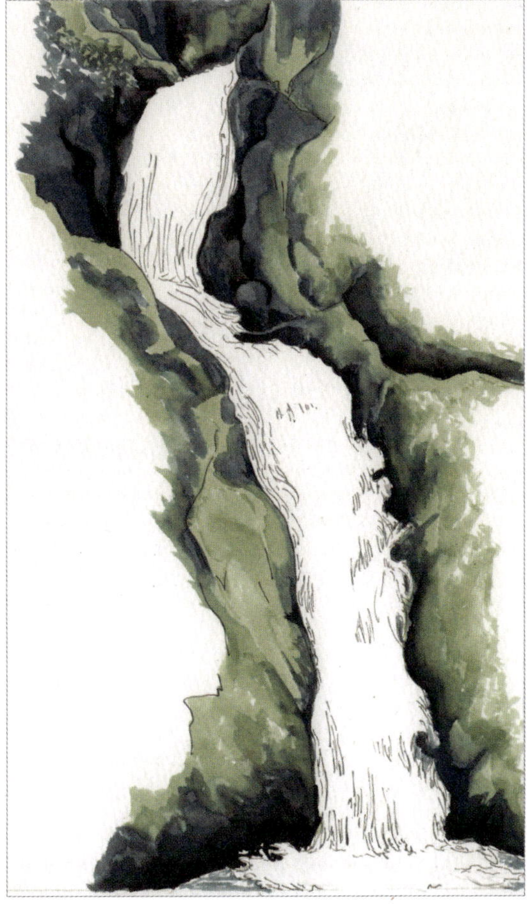

Lesson 7

A Mature River

By the time the river reaches the lowlands, it has usually widened and deepened dramatically. The centre of the river is fast-moving, but because of the depth of the water, it appears sedate. The character of the river varies significantly depending on its interaction with the surrounding environment.

Humans have always been drawn to rivers as sources of water to drink, wash in, carry away waste, and facilitate transport. Today, the vast majority of people live in cities or large towns, close to a water source. The urban river comes with its special features, not least the architectural wonders of modern bridges.

Capturing the environment of the urban river presents its own challenges. In this exercise, we will look at drawing bridges and shading the water of the mature river in coloured pencil, building on the water colourscape exercises of Lesson 3.

Additional materials:

Ruler, burnisher pencil

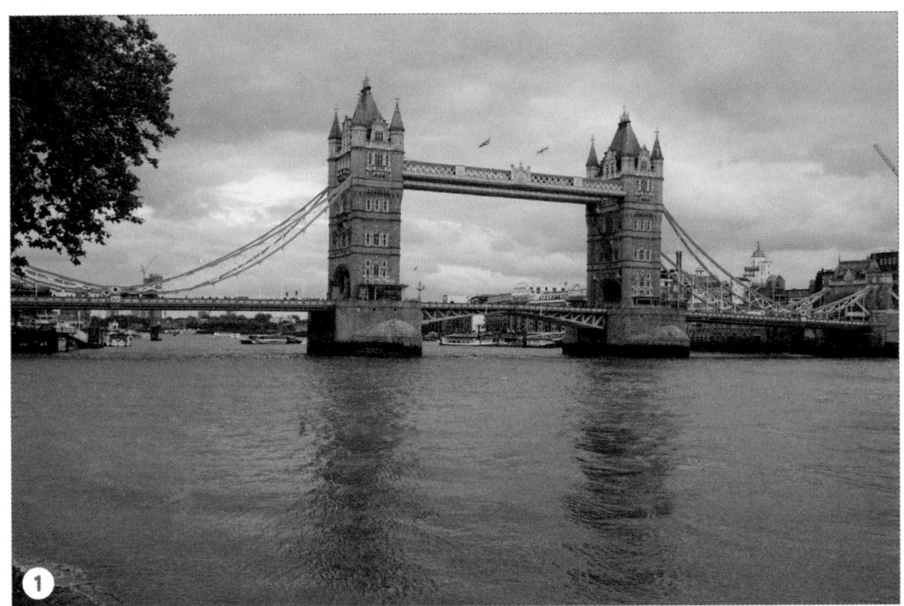

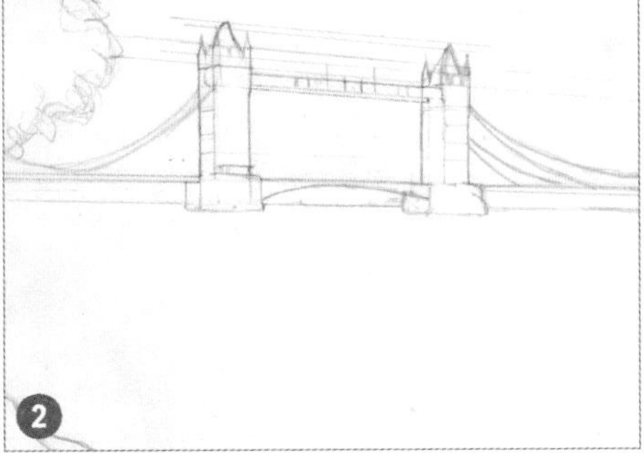

❶ Use a reference photo of an urban site with a bridge that spans your chosen river. If there is no urban setting, find an image or photograph that you can work from. This example uses a very famous location – Tower Bridge in London.

❷ Begin with a graphite sketch. Bridges pose a few challenges with perspective and a ruler may help when placing your image square onto the paper. First, ensure the image is straight relative to your paper, then lay your ruler across a straight line on the bridge on your reference image. Now draw along the ruler at the same angle onto your paper. Repeat for all the main lines on the bridge and you will have a framework to work from. If you wish, you could continue these lines to help locate the vanishing point and improve perspective throughout the drawing.

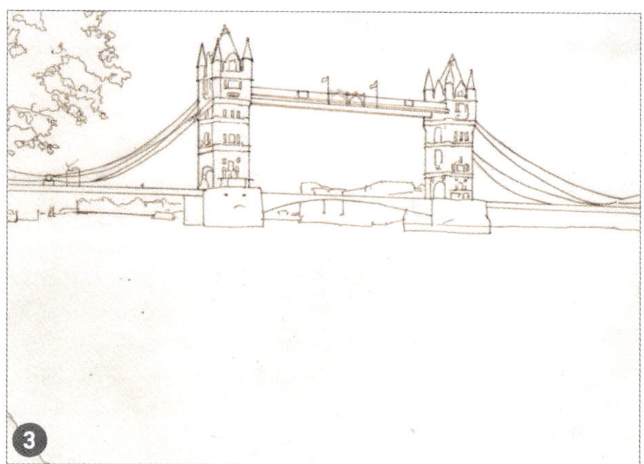

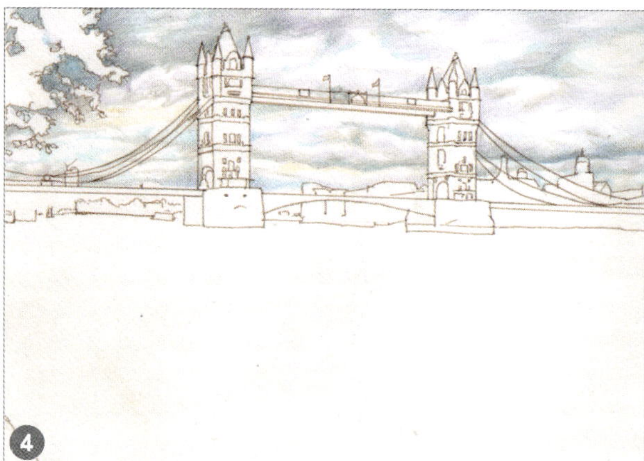

Tip:

Remember that not all of the page needs to be covered; leaving some areas the colour of the paper can increase contrast and enhance the image.

❸ As an option, you could use a fineliner to outline the main structure and bank elements. I chose a sepia fineliner here as I did not wish the lines to show up strongly in the final, coloured image. Avoid drawing any lines into the river itself, as colour will be used to generate water movement and reflections.

❹ Begin by colouring the sky, getting the entirety of the work done in this part of the image all at the same time. I used a mixture of colours: light blue, lavender purple, Payne's grey, and yellow ochre to add hints of warm light into the clouds. Much of the cloud was left the colour of the paper.

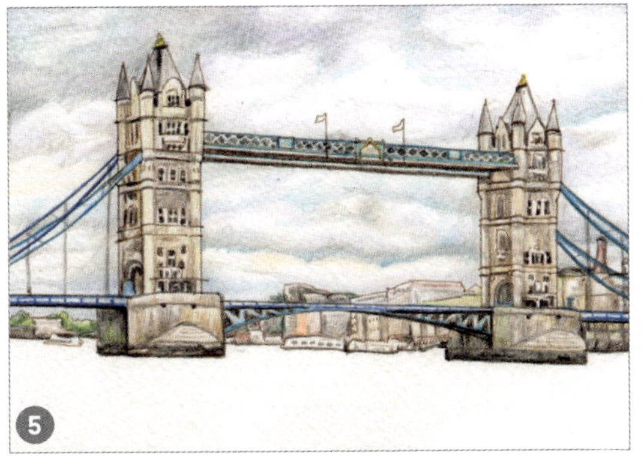

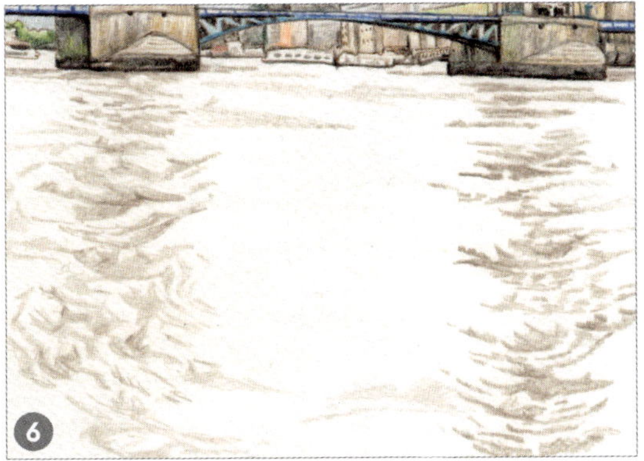

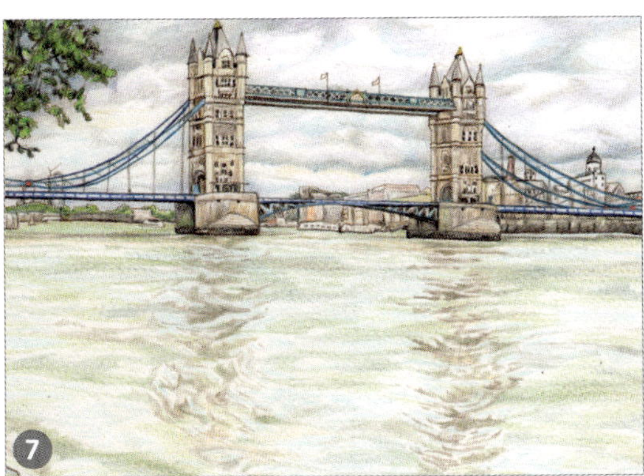

5 Next, work on the bridge itself. As much as possible, work into your drawing from top to bottom and left to right (if right-handed) or right to left (if left-handed). As with the graphite scene in Lesson 5, avoid revisiting areas that are finished. Use sharp pencils to fill in details. Always keep the main subject of the drawing in mind. In this case, I focused on the bridge and the water, so that the bridge is much more detailed than the bankside buildings in the background.

6 The river itself deserves special focus. When composing the scene, take note of elements of interest and variety of colour or shape that can be brought out in the water. Here, the reflection of the bridge is of prime importance. Using burnt umber, I drew in the reflected patterns of the towers. Do the same for your river image, using the darkest colour that you can identify.

7 Continue to build up the layers, working outwards from the darkest colour that you put down in the previous step. Seek interesting colours within the water in your photo and consider slightly exaggerating them. I chose to emphasise the yellow ochre and olive green in the water of the River Thames. Continue to blend colours into the water until you reach a point that you are happy with.

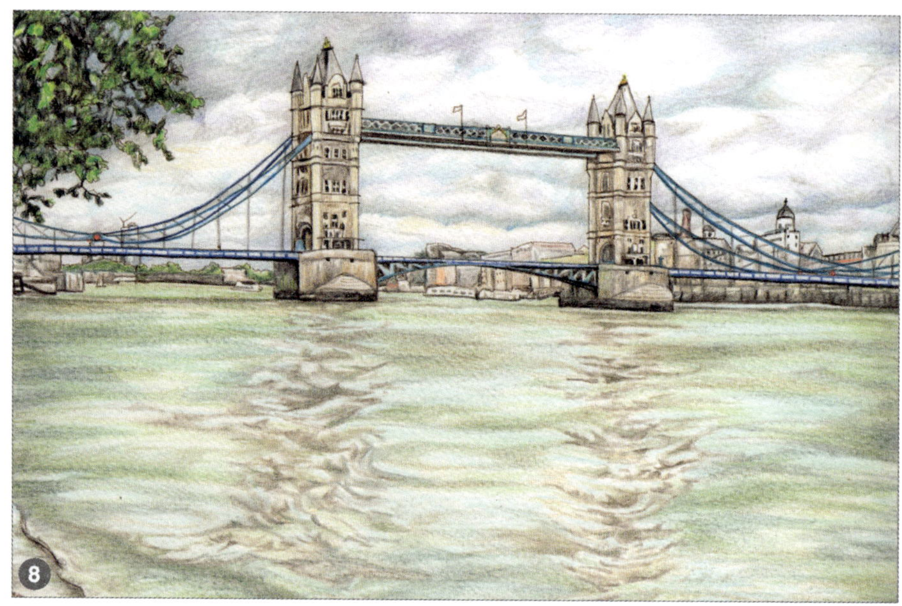

8 Consider giving the water a final layer of a special wax "burnisher" pencil to blend the colours together and give the drawing a consistent, smooth finish. A light colour from your set (white, pale yellow, pale green, or pale blue) can be used in place of a burnisher pencil if you don't have one.

Gallery

In this coloured pencil drawing of Southwark Bridge, further upstream from Tower Bridge in London, I focused even more on density of colour in the river greatly enhancing the colour range visible in the water, which has been exaggerated and brightened from the reference image. Such colour choices can be used to cheer a somewhat dreary image. I also chose to avoid using too much ruler in this small image, giving a more organic cast to the buildings.

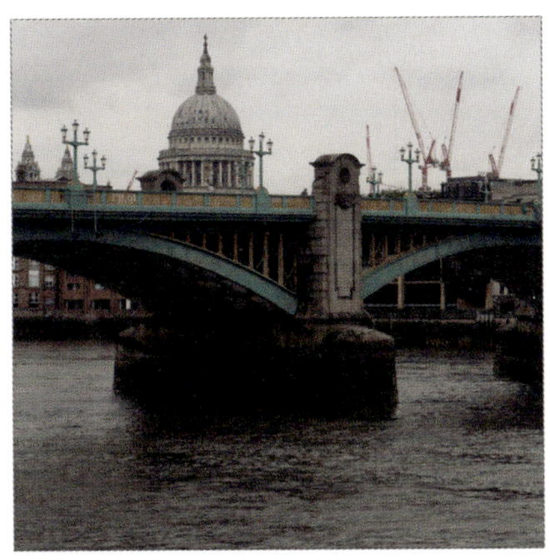

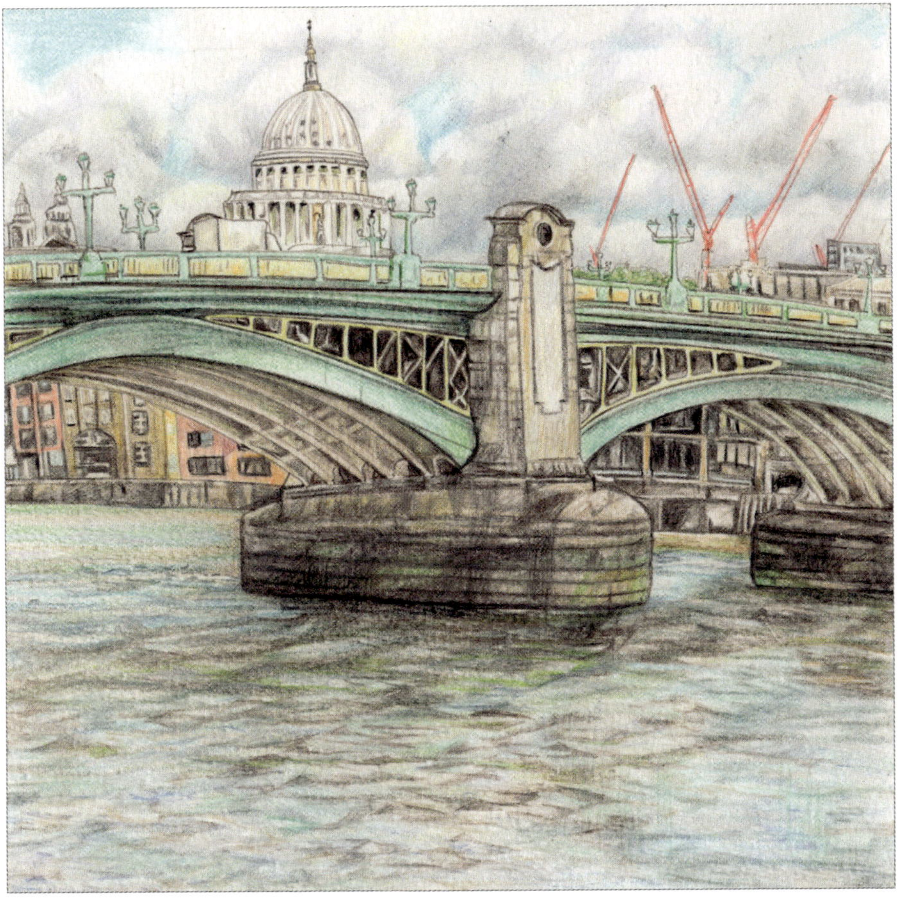

Lesson 8

A Tidal River

By the time the river reaches its end point (usually the sea) it is wide and expansive. It deposits great volumes of suspended material each low tide as it loses energy when the sea retreats. This creates features such as mudflats and deltas, and gives the river estuary an interesting and unique landscape.

Estuaries and mudflats are often fascinating natural environments that are full of life. If it is possible to visit the estuary of your river, take your nature journal and record and photograph the wildlife that you see there.

In this exercise, we will look at the estuary environment using a new colouring technique with ink brush pens. If you don't have brush pens, the same idea can be emulated in most colour media, including coloured pencil. The most important aspect of this technique, and what gives it such an interesting style, is that every colour is laid independently without blending. This gives an effect that resembles printing, despite being drawn by hand.

Additional materials:

Ink brush pens

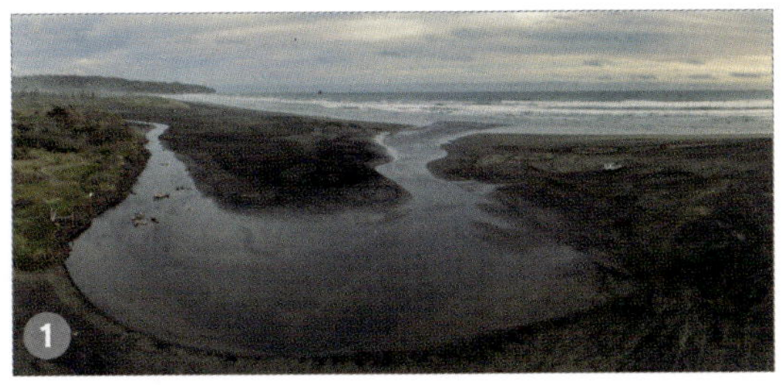

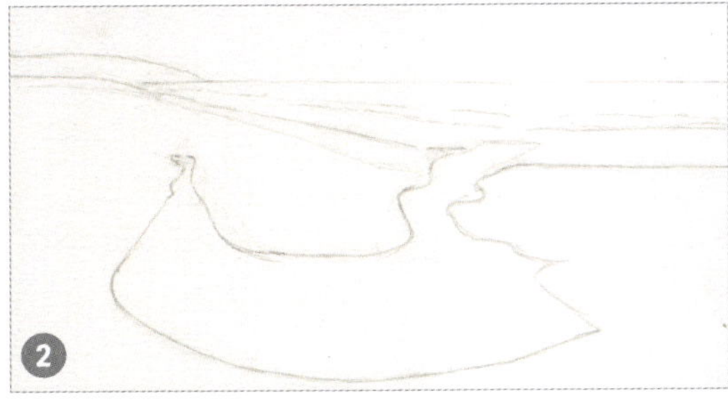

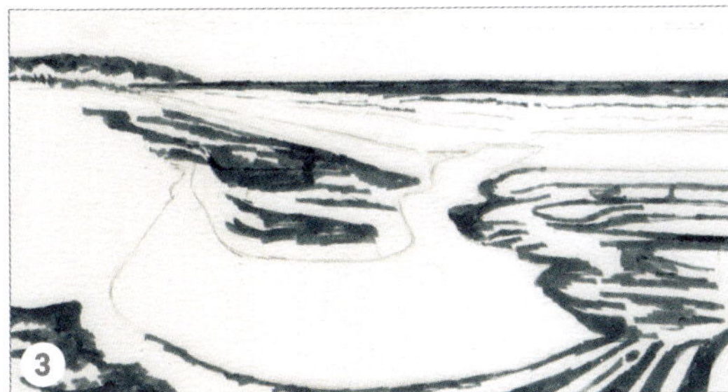

❶ Use a reference photo of an estuary or mudflat environment, from your own project river if possible. In this example, I am using an aerial angled photo of an estuary in Auckland, New Zealand. For an alternative, standard ground-level view, see the Gallery example of my local river. Either aerial or ground-level photos are suitable for this exercise. You could even use a satellite image (such as Google Earth) – for more on this idea see Lesson 13.

❷ Begin with a graphite sketch of the main features of the estuary scene, breaking it down into a shorthand of shapes and outlines. When you are happy with your drawing, use an eraser to "knock back" the pencil lines so they are only just visible. This will avoid the lines interfering with your colouring, especially since one of the features of this approach is leaving some areas the colour of the paper.

❸ This technique gets its interesting style from laying a single colour at a time, with no blending between layers. Select one colour that is common across your reference photo – you may need to simplify the colour range. Lay this colour down everywhere that you see it.

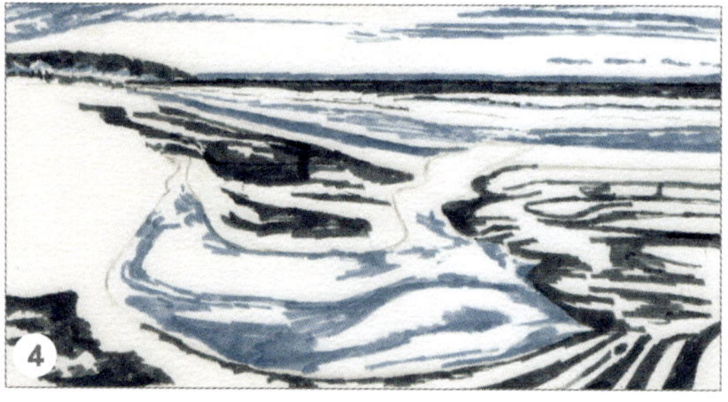

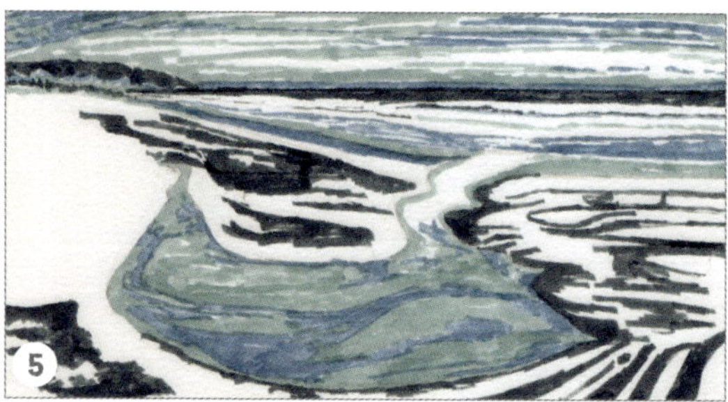

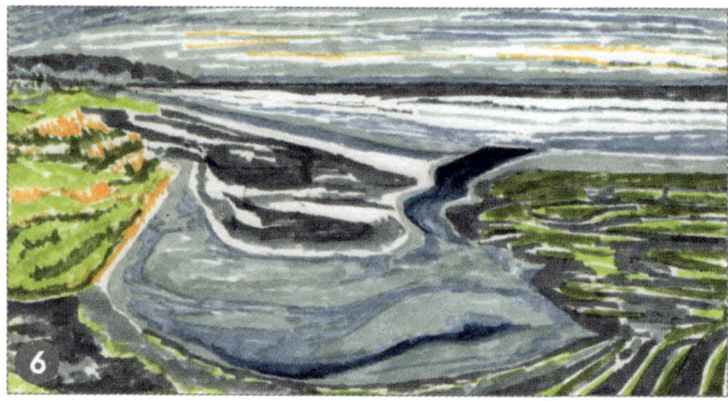

4 Now select a second colour and do the same, laying it down in separate areas and avoiding overlapping colours. This can be particularly effective if areas of white are left between the different colours.

5 Continue to add colours. I have kept to a blue palette for these first few stages, slightly varying the shade. One of the advantages of an ink brush pen is the variety of paintbrush marks that can be created. Rather than aiming for solid blocks of colour, I deliberately emphasised the brush marks and allowed them to remain visible.

6 I have added a couple more colours here: two different greens and a yellow ochre, for the foreground marshes. A few areas of white still remain but the majority are now being filled in.

TIP:

If you are using a medium that will smudge, lay a spare sheet of paper under your hand.

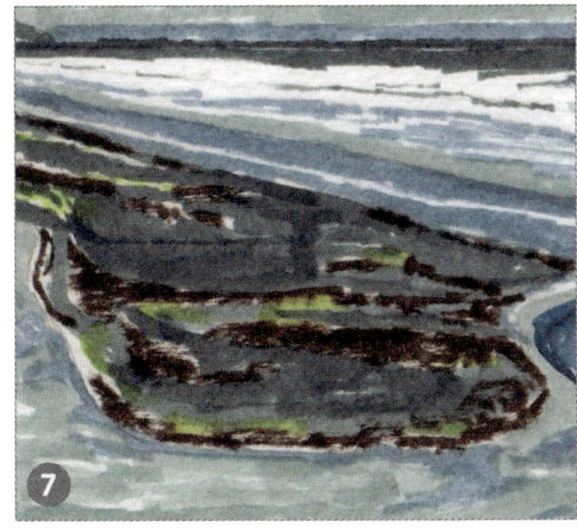

7 The bias of my colours was in the yellow and blue range with very little red, so a touch of reddish brown was added as a final colour. This red was mainly used as a substitute for black and dark brown, as I intended to minimise very dark layers in this particular drawing to allow the marks made in the next stage to be visible.

8 Finally, a thick black fineliner (size 1.2) was used to add loose marks over the top, defining the main areas of the image, such as the edges of the river, the horizon, and the sweeping lines across the estuary that were present in the reference image.

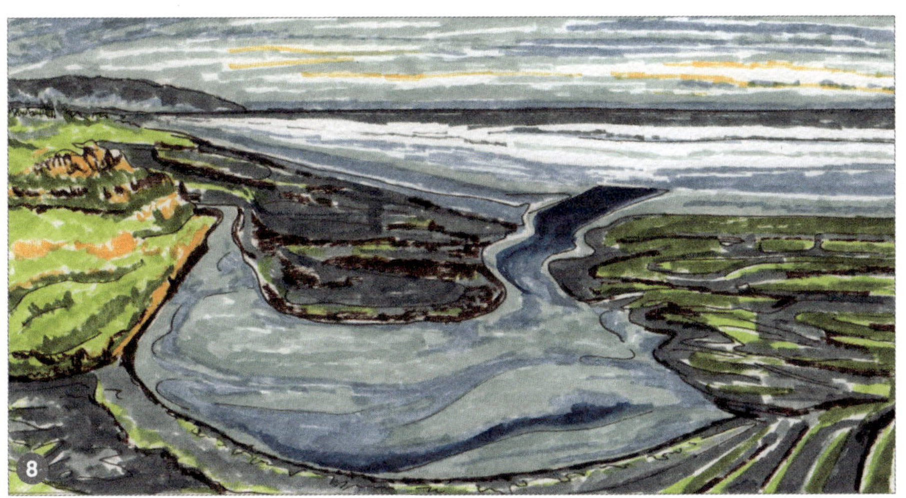

Gallery

You can add as many or as few colours as you like when working this way, and make more or less of the final black line stage. In this scene of my local estuary, I decided to incorporate some of my nature journal sketches and photographs in the final layer. Once the colouring stage had been done, thick fineliner and a black ink brush pen were used to add the birds.

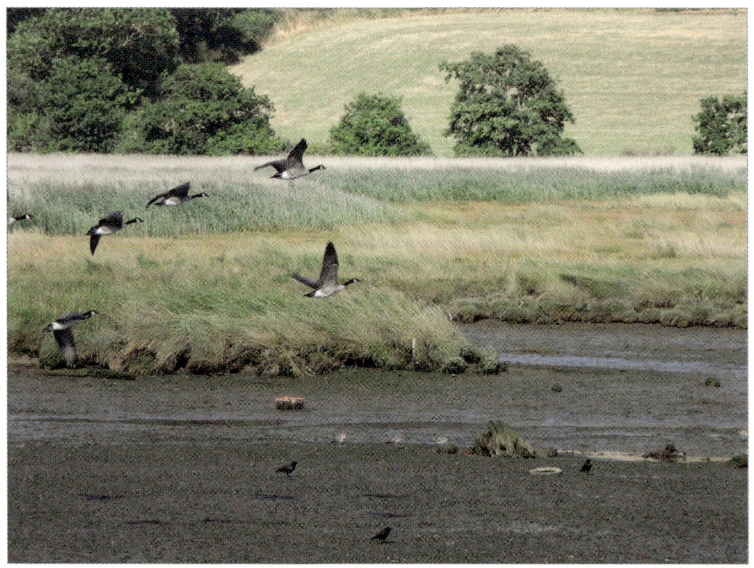

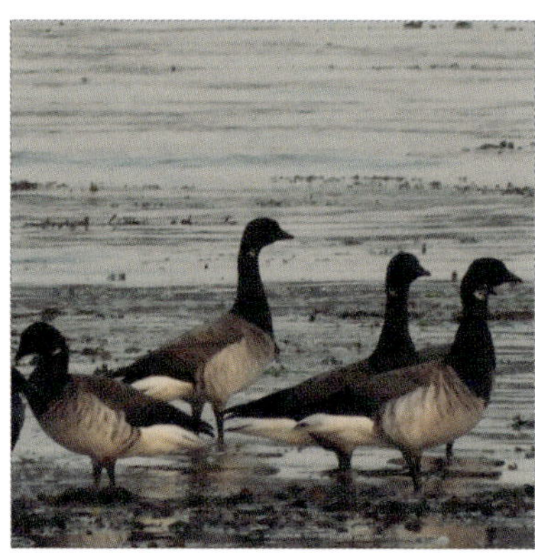

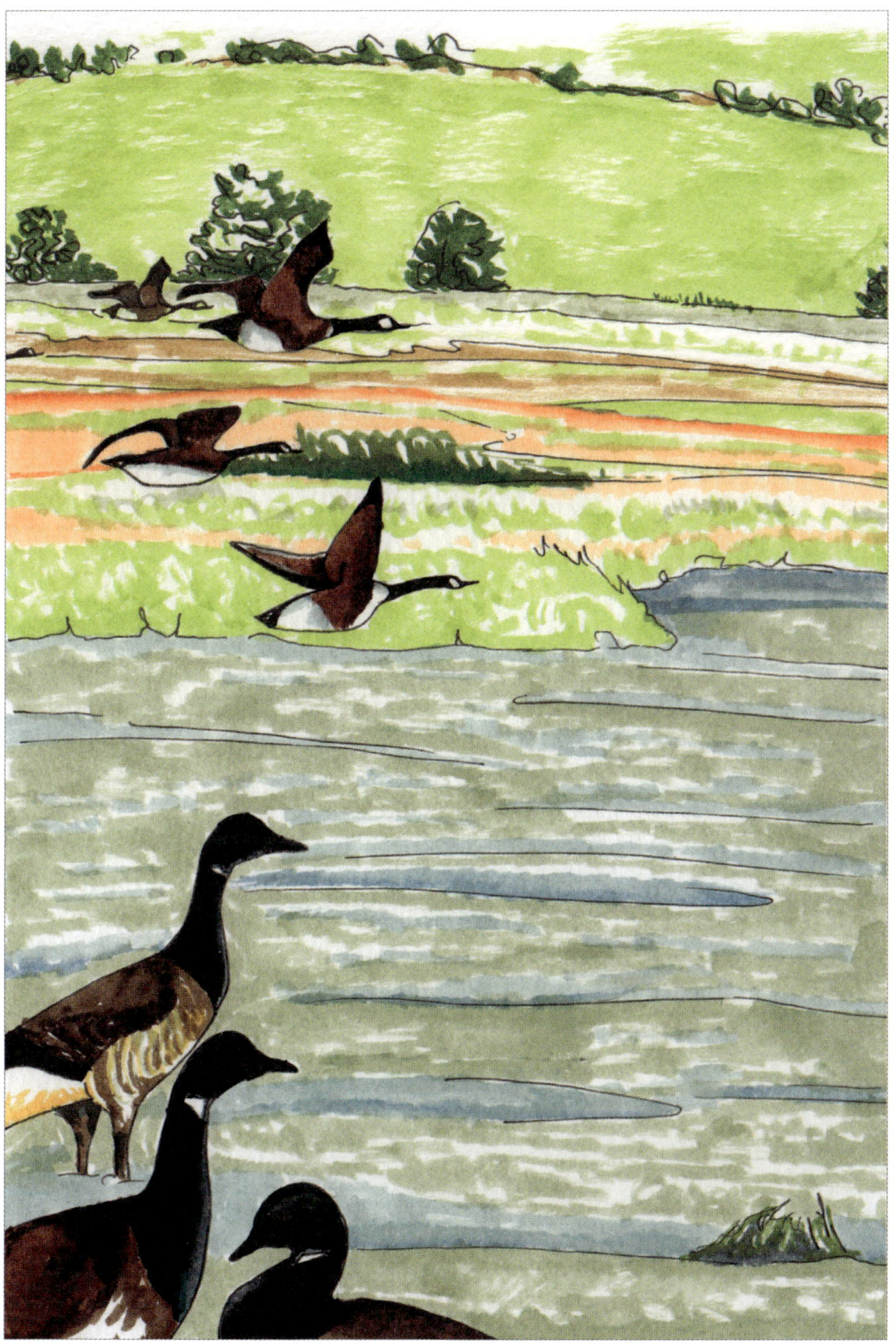

Chapter 3

River Dwellers

So far, we have looked at the river itself, its changing surface and interaction with the landscape. In this chapter we will focus on the inhabitants of a river, from birds and insects to fish and humans. You will learn to capture sketches of wildlife, working outdoors to hone your skills at sketching in the field, and using reference photos to build the detail in your journal back at home.

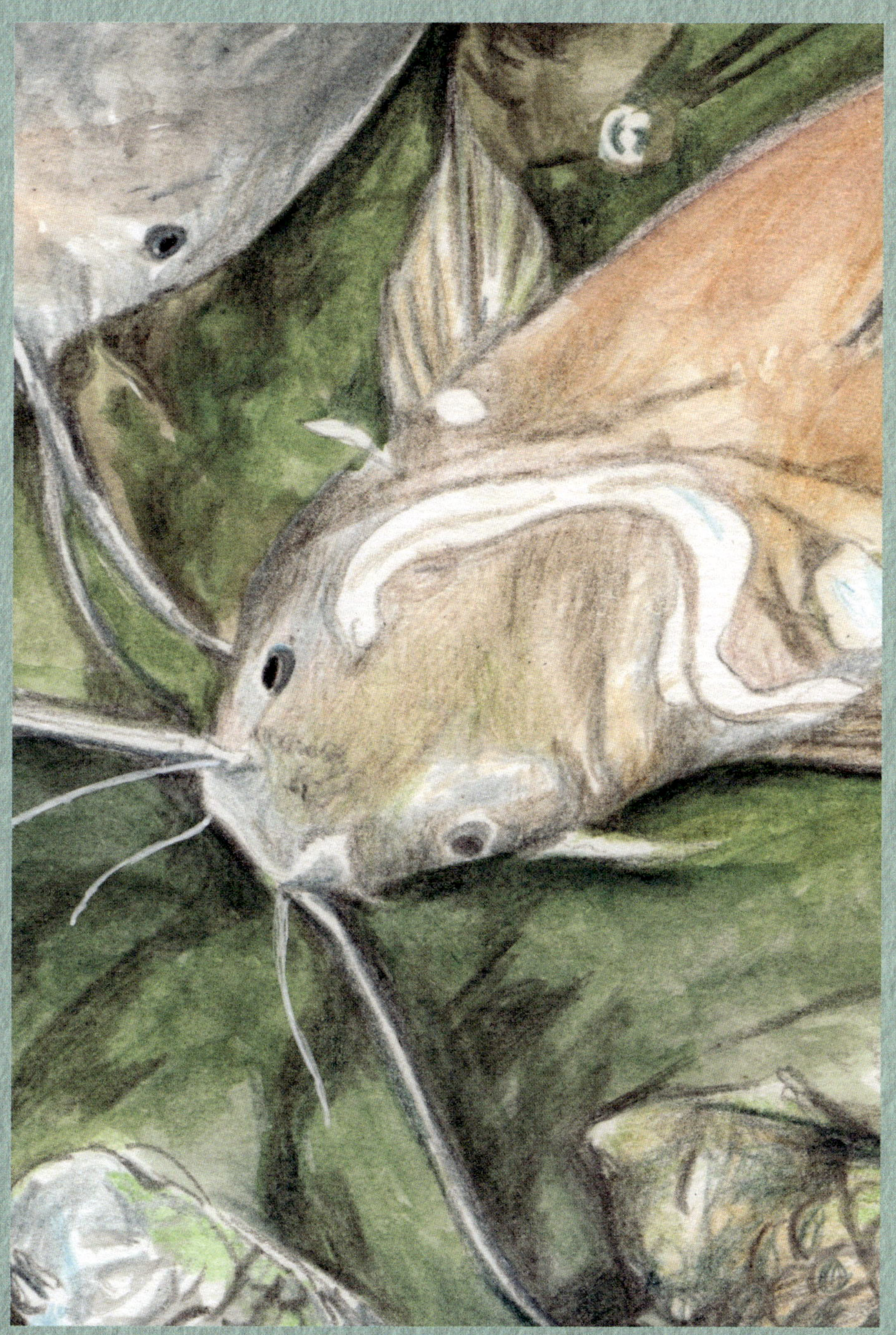

Lesson 9

Sketching Birds

Rivers, from source to sea, are excellent habitats for a great range of waterfowl. Very often vegetative corridors are allowed to remain along riverbanks, and these margins also support many land birds. River-dwelling fowl include gulls, ducks, waders, divers, kingfishers, and a whole host of other interesting birds adapted to the water environment.

Most birds are unlikely to remain sufficiently still to sketch easily, but some river birds, such as ducks, gulls, and waders, make excellent models for outdoor sketching due to their grazing habit and relative tolerance of humans, which means they will generally remain in place long enough for at least a photograph.

In this lesson, I will show you two methods for quickly sketching birds in the field, or from a video or photograph. It is most important with field sketching to get used to making rapid marks and embrace mistakes. For quick progress, try sketching pages of birds without allowing yourself access to an eraser.

The Line Method

❶ If you can, begin with some ducks or gulls, or any other river bird that you can access easily, and get a few photographs to work from. If possible, try this method outdoors, or begin your practice from photos and progress to the riverbank.

❷ Start with the top of the bird's head through to the tip of its tail. Get used to drawing this in a fluid gesture, a single line if you can. Don't be afraid to fill a whole page with "duck back lines".

❸ Add the head and beak. Concentrate on the head position, the angle of the beak, and position of the eye. Again, you could fill a page with duck heads and necks. Get used to observing how the bird moves its head, and the angles made when the neck crosses the bird's body.

❹ Now add the rest of the body. Look at the shape of the line from under the beak down under the belly to the tail. As before, try to draw this in a fluid line, similar to an elongated "S". Practise drawing bird shapes in as few marks as possible. Add the position of the legs.

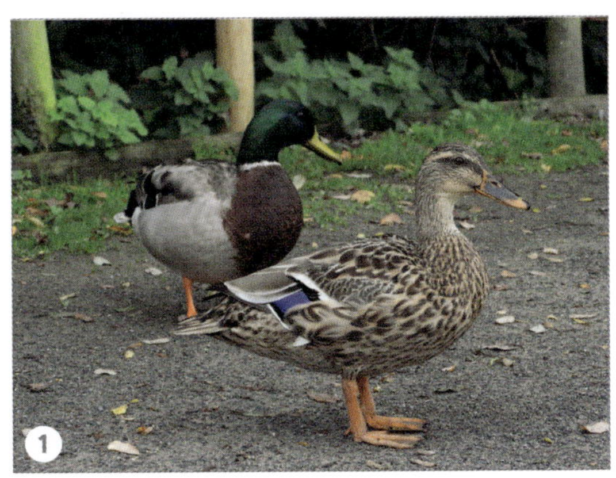

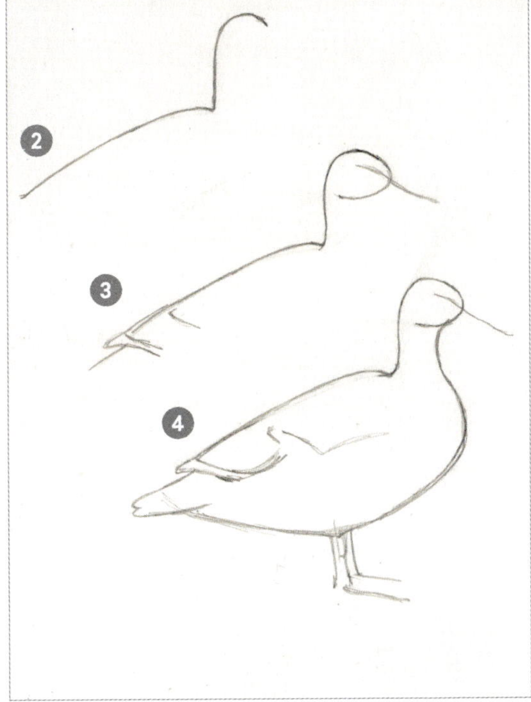

TIP:

Try taking a video of your birds to draw from. This is a great halfway point between a still photograph and a live bird who may fly away at any time. Put the video on loop and sketch away, knowing the bird will soon return to the same position!

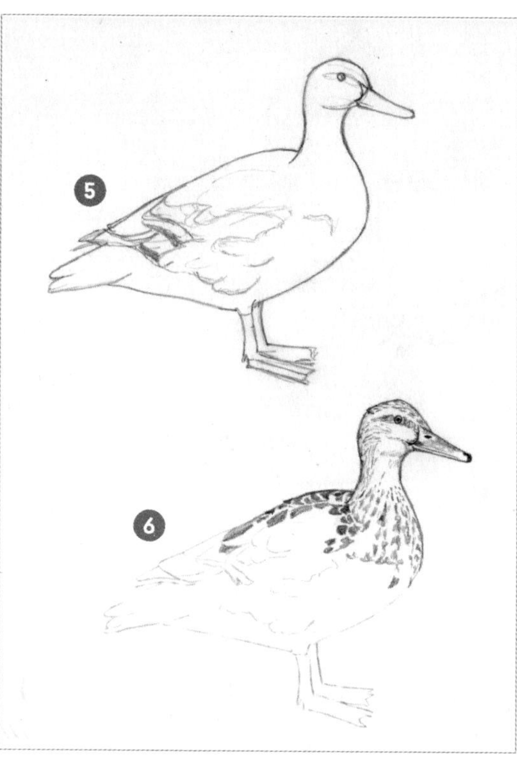

5 If you have more time with your bird, or are working from a photograph, you can start to fill in more details. Note the shape of the beak, details in the eye, and the positions of the main banks of feathers in the wing, marking the outline of the main areas of colour change.

6 With a little more time, you can add full details, just as you would with a graphite landscape. Begin with the face and mark in the plumage patterns, working down the neck to the shoulders and wings. Are the patterns mottled, barred, or spotted? How do the feathers change shape in the wings compared to the down on the body?

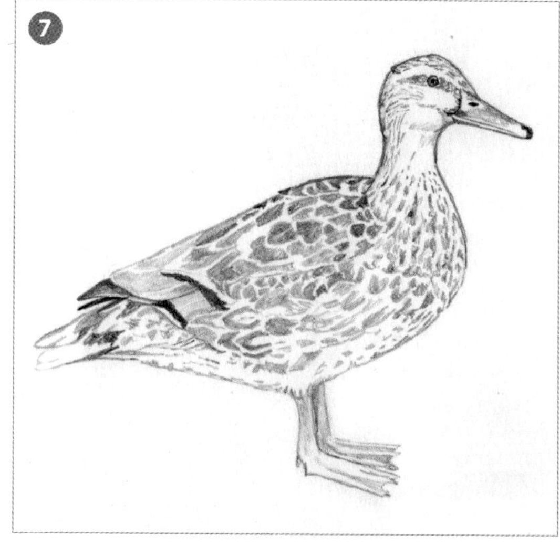

7 Continue until you have added detail to the entire sketch. Don't let this take too long, as these are just quick sketches intended to improve your observational skills, rather than works of art on their own.

The Shape Method

❶ For some birds or positions, the "line method" just doesn't make the most sense for beginning a sketch. For example, this heron is hunkered down, and from this angle you really can't see the top of the head and back in isolation.

❷ Instead of the line method, begin by lightly drawing the overall shape of the bird's body. I simplified this heron into an oval with a pointed end, held at an angle by a vertical leg. Position the head and legs onto your initial shape with simple directional marks.

❸ Now fill in some of the bird's features. Draw in the main areas of different colours on the plumage and thicken out the indications of legs, beak, and eye. You can make these marks more confident and a little darker on top of your softly drawn shape sketch.

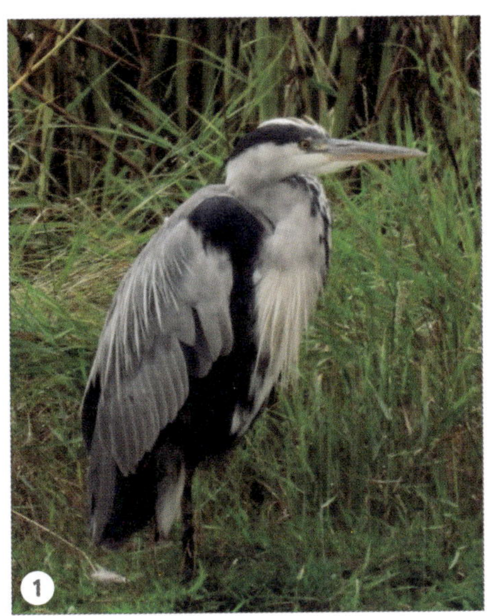

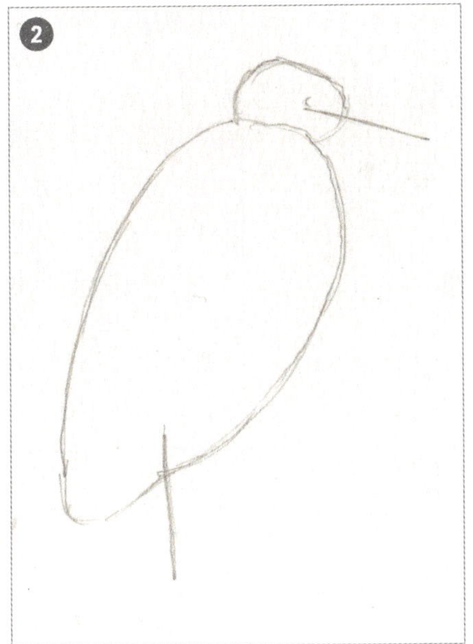

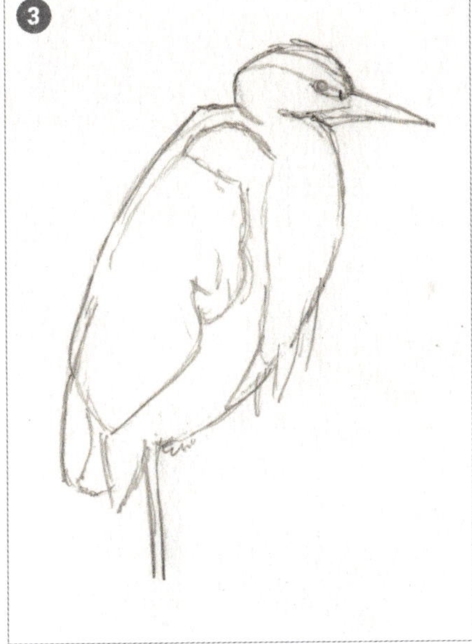

❹ Continue to fill in details, such as the positions of the main feathers. Keep checking your earlier lines; I decided to thicken up the bird's head and adjust the angle of the back of the body.

❺ Finally, add in a little shading to the dark areas, and some marks to indicate texture such as the shaggy contour feathers of this bird's breast. As before, don't spend too long before you move on to a new position – several loose sketches will improve your skills faster than a few sketches in exquisite detail.

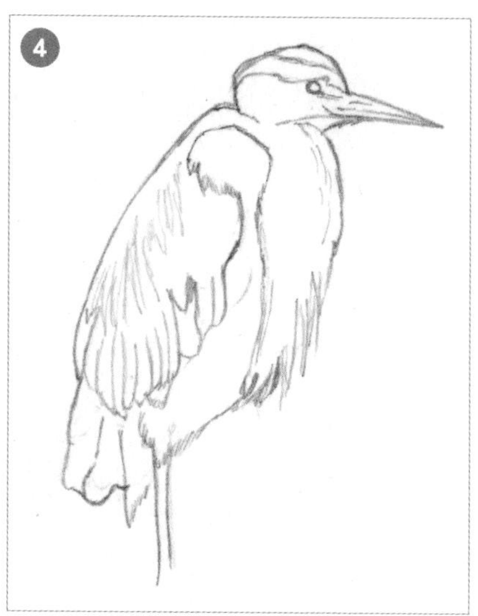

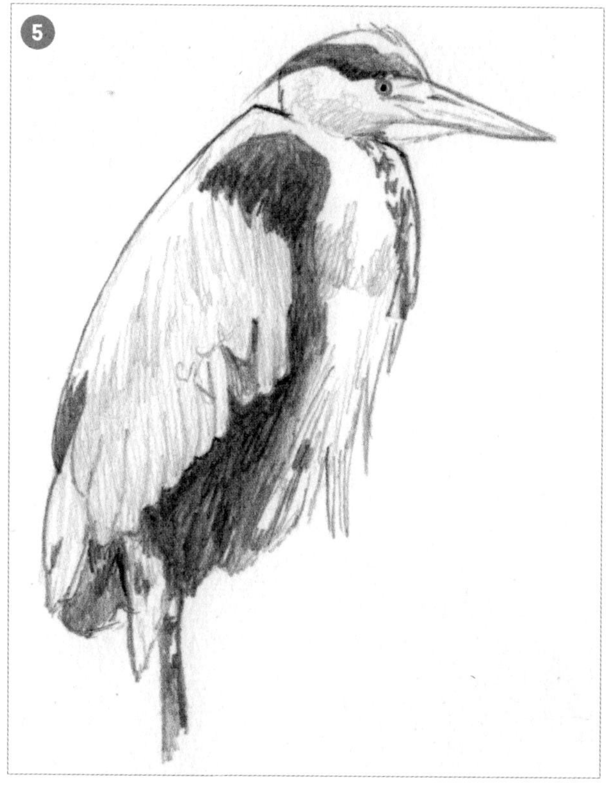

Gallery

Getting out as often as you can to draw birds by the river will increase your skills. Filling pages with quick sketches like these is ideal. To make the pages look effective, vary the amount of detail in each sketch, with a few examples receiving a little more attention, and ensure that the birds have different postures and face in different directions across each page. Sketch them from the side, above, feeding, sleeping, wading, and in the water.

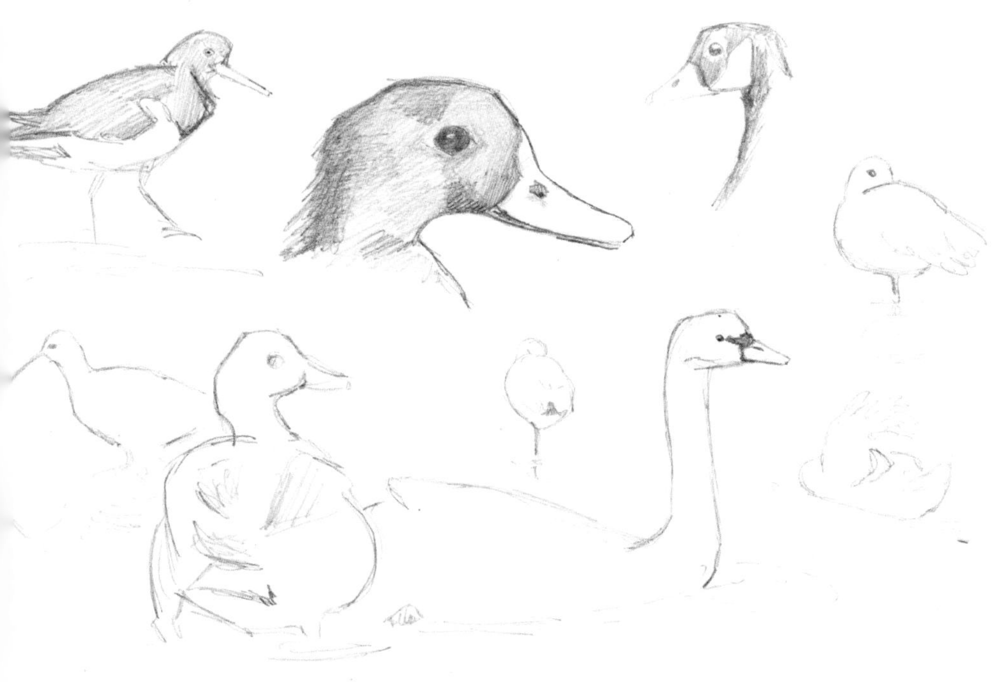

Lesson 10

Drawing Boats

People are, of course, the most prominent river dweller in almost all rivers. Humans have the capability to create river crossings, change the river course, add or remove obstructions, and alter the river environment. People also move on the river surface, using boats for business or pleasure. These boats, and the people that use them, are the focus of our next fineliner lesson.

Boats come in an enormous range of shapes and sizes. The types of boat present on your river will be so entangled with the human and physical geography of the river and its surroundings, that just surveying the boats and their purposes would be a research project itself. As artists, seeking out interesting boats to draw will be our main priority. Once you are comfortable sketching the boats in isolation, they can be added to your wider river landscape practice.

This lesson is all about first getting the graphite sketch right, then using fineliner techniques to add linework and detail to the boat drawings. The inclusion of human figures and a splash of colour will also be covered here.

1 Select some interesting boats to work on. For obvious reasons, boats are more likely to be present where the river is mature and deep, and are especially found clustered around human population centres and the estuary. Choose at least three boats to begin with and take photographs.

2 I usually start drawing a boat by putting down as much as is visible of the inside as a single shape. If the inside is not visible, skip to the next step to begin sketching the hull.

3 Add the shape of the visible hull and the line of the water. Capturing the perspective of these linear shapes is important. As for the bridge in Lesson 7, you could use a ruler with your reference photograph to help you visualise and transfer all the different angles to your drawing.

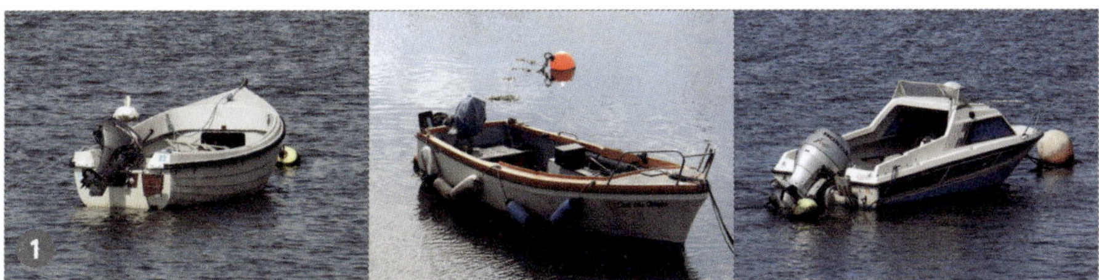

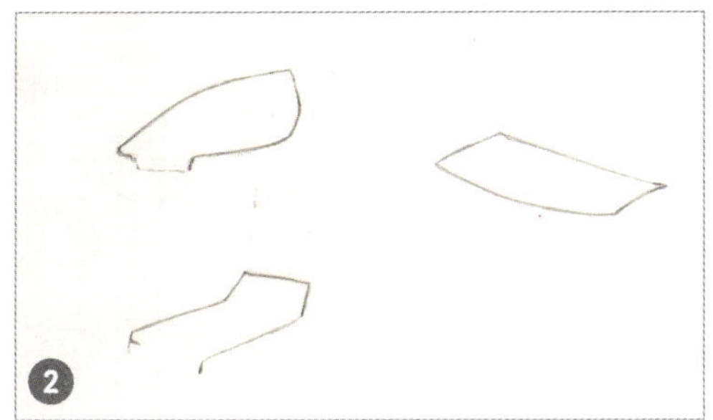

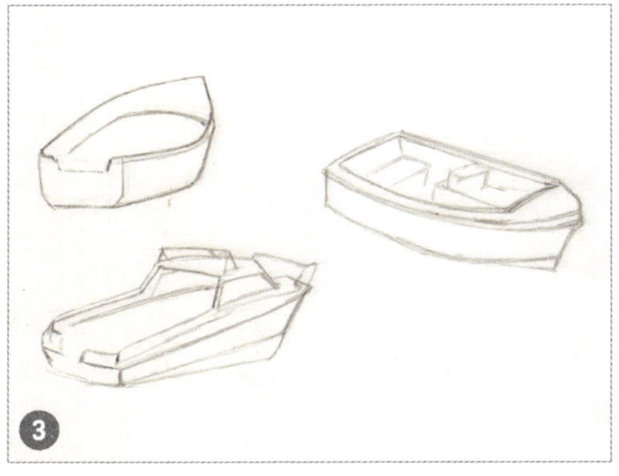

TIP:

Gesture the shape. When drawing the curves of boat hulls, look at the photo and imagine yourself drawing the line before putting pencil to paper. You might even draw it in the air with a finger. You'll be surprised how effective this is for getting the shape of the line into your pencil.

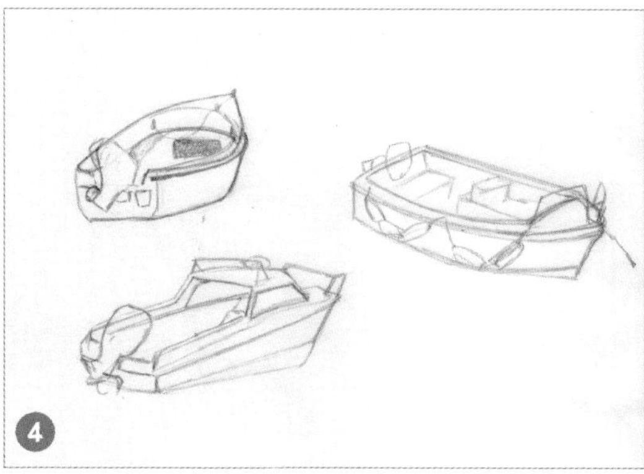

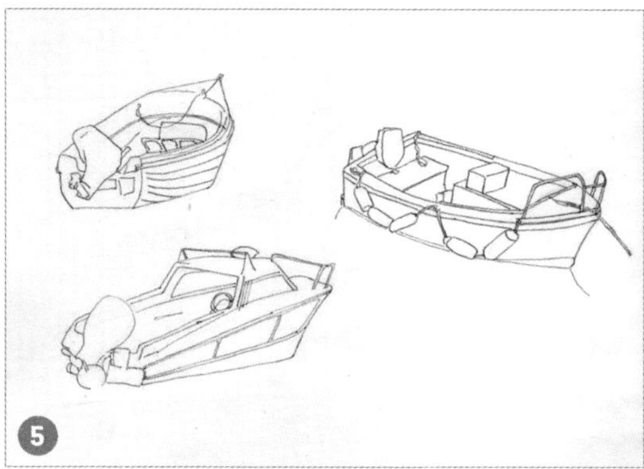

❹ Still using your pencil, note the positions of the main elements of the boat without shading or excessive levels of detail. For these seafaring estuary boats, I focused on the hanging buoys, the ropes, and the engines.

❺ Once you are satisfied with the graphite sketch, move to the fineliner. I started with a size 0.2 fineliner; a thinner nib is best at this stage – you can always make lines thicker. Once you have finished, remove the pencil sketch below with a pointed or battery-operated eraser.

❻ Select some lines to thicken. Linework drawings usually look best if the line thickness is not uniform. Choose lines that are in shadow, or that represent an important part of the boat that you wish to emphasise. From here you may wish to add some shading (cross-hatching or ink brush pen) or colour to the linework (see Gallery, overleaf).

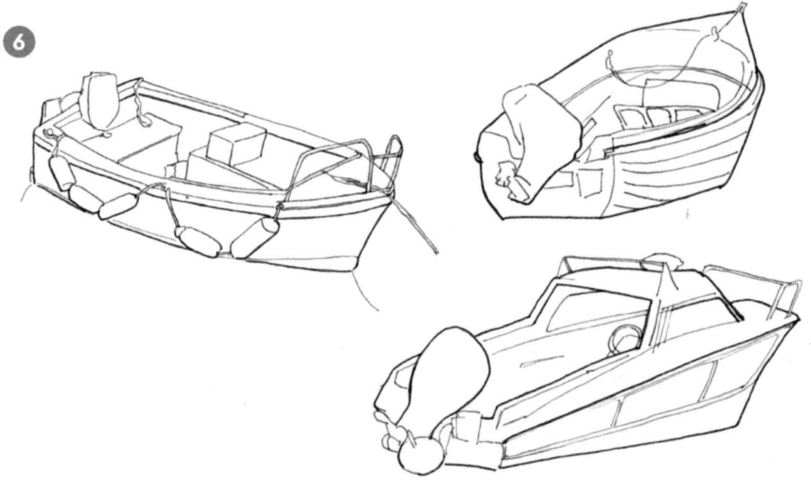

Human Figures

If you spot someone out on the river, you might want to include a human figure in your boat drawing. Go about this in a similar way, sketching the human figure roughly in graphite at the first stage of the drawing.

- *You can simplify a human figure into head, torso, arms, and legs.*
- *Notice the angles of each of these components independently.*
- *Avoid getting carried away with high levels of detail as the general shape will be enough to indicate the human form.*
- *When you are happy, add linework and shading.*

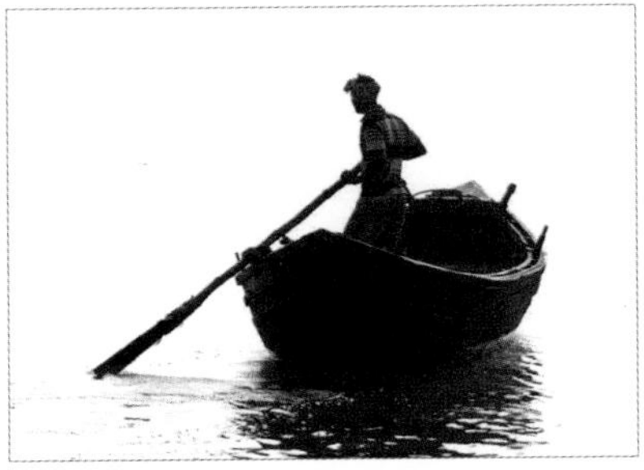

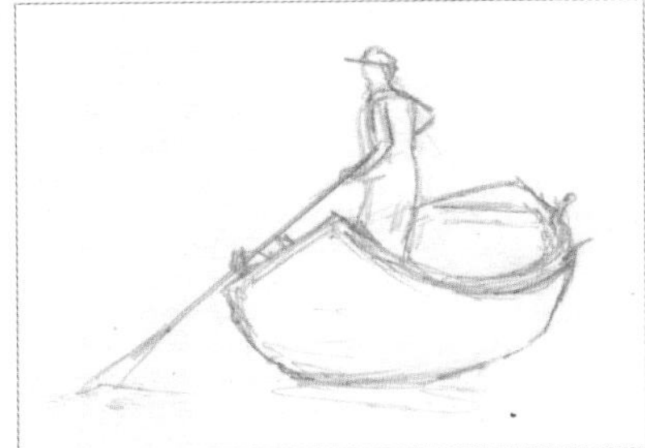

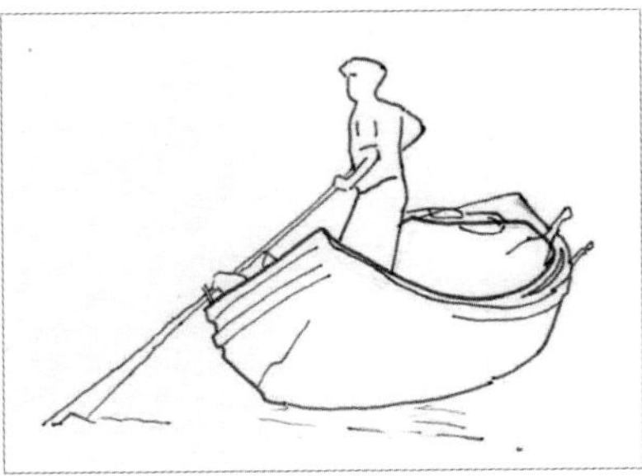

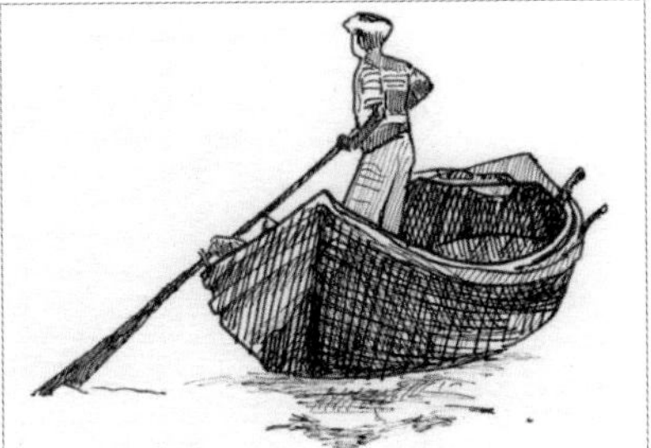

Gallery

These images show the variety of water crafts and their operatives. Shading or colour has been added to these sketches. A combination of both colour and cross-hatching can be very effective; use the cross-hatching to bring most of the shading and detail but lay a little colour over the top to add some vibrancy. The choice of whether to shade, colour, do both, or leave the sketch as linework is entirely yours.

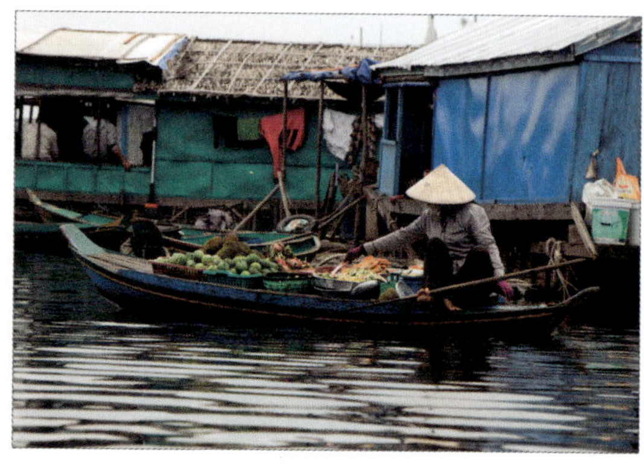

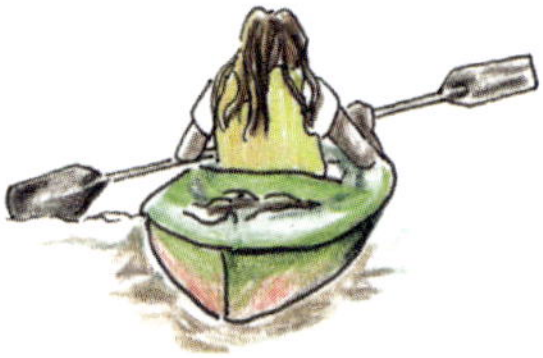

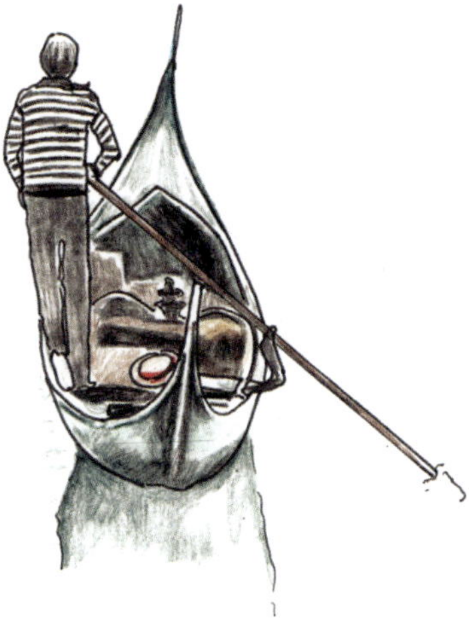

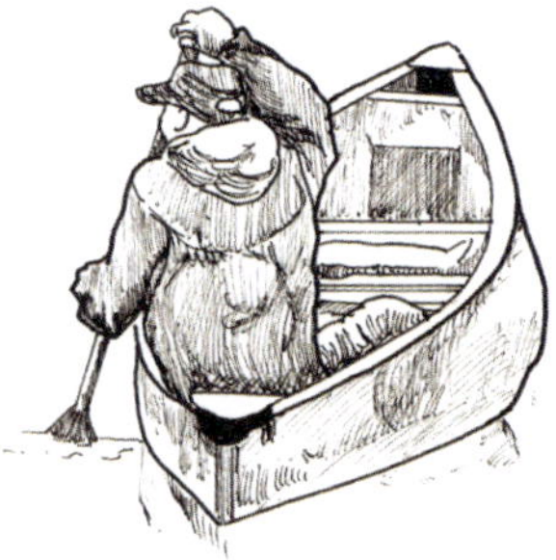

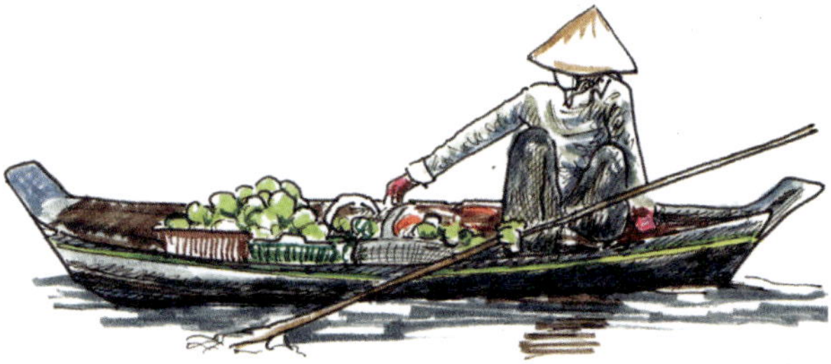

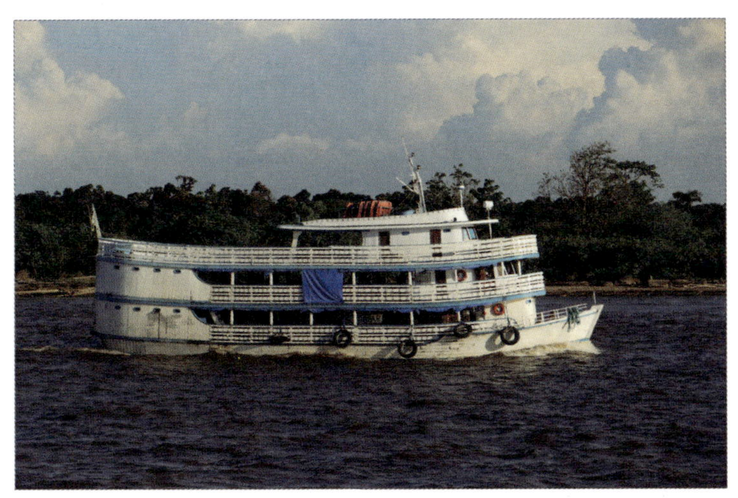

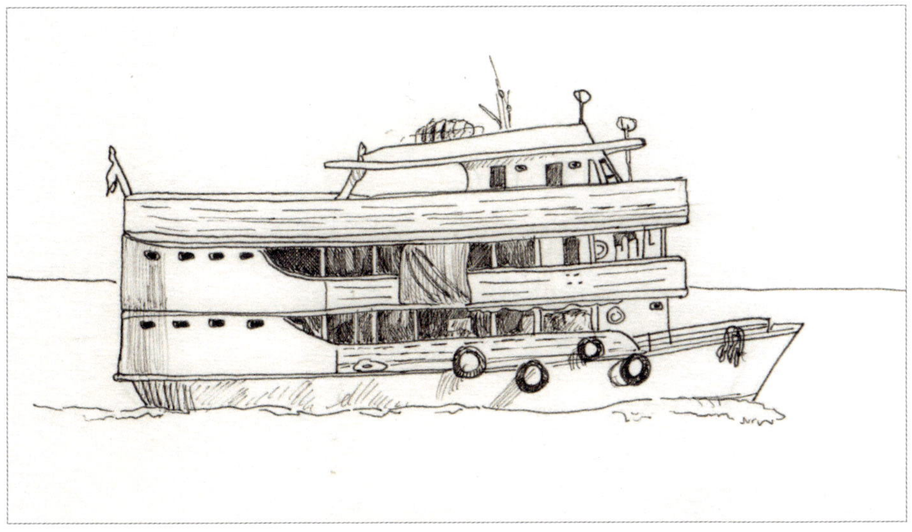

Lesson 11

Insect Life

Water-dwelling insects are fascinating, with many interesting species, such as dragonflies and mayflies, having an aquatic stage in their life cycle. River edges also support thousands of land and flying insects such as bees, butterflies, moths, wasps, and flies. There is so much to be discovered about the insect life along your river, if you are willing to take up the task.

You might decide to include a more focused search for insects on one of your river visits, or just note down in your walk log or nature journal anything that you spot as you pass by. Take photos when you can for sketching – some advice is provided opposite. Some excellent smartphone apps and field guidebooks are available to help you identify the species you find.

Coloured pencil is a great medium for sketching insects as you can use the bright colours and sharp points to bring out the intricate details of an insect form. In this exercise, we will look at using sharp coloured pencils to recreate the bright colours of damselfly wings. Examine the technique used here and see if you can apply it to an insect subject of your own.

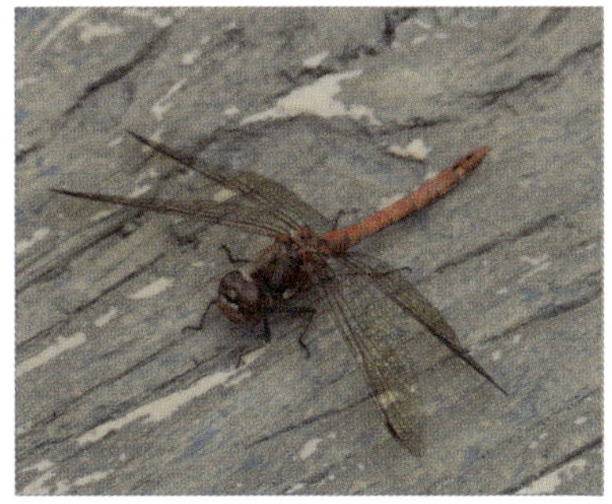

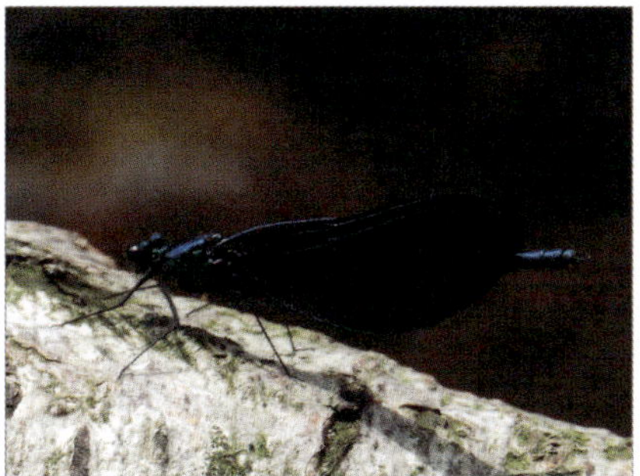

Insect Photography

You will need a certain amount of patience and perseverance to take photos of insects. While photographing them in flight might require specialist equipment, waiting for them to land and settle will provide a brief window of opportunity. Butterflies and bees are relatively easy to capture when they are busy searching for nectar, and other insects, such as spiders, may also be snapped as they pause on webs or foliage by the water.

- *A smartphone is enough to take some wonderful insect photos. Avoid zooming in too far as this will make your photo blurry. Keep your finger ready to tap for focus and instead approach for a closer shot. Some camera apps also have a "macro/close-up" mode.*
- *Settled insects such as dragonflies and butterflies quickly escape when you come close. A distant photo is often better than none at all. As you approach, take a photo with each step. You can then keep the closest photo you were able to get and delete the rest.*
- *When approaching the insect, try not to allow your shadow to cross its path. Many insects will not detect you if you approach towards the sun and tread lightly.*

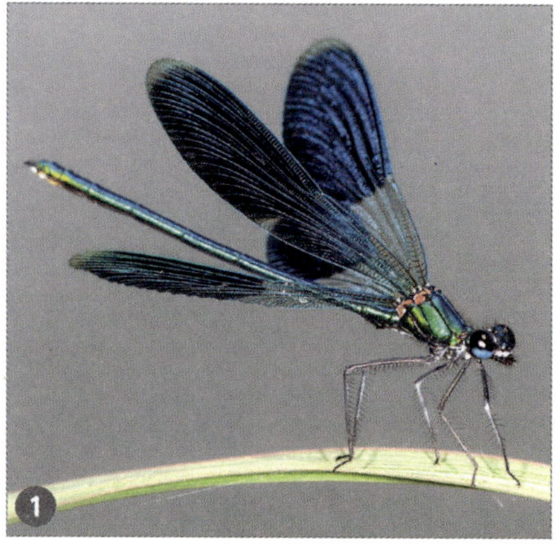

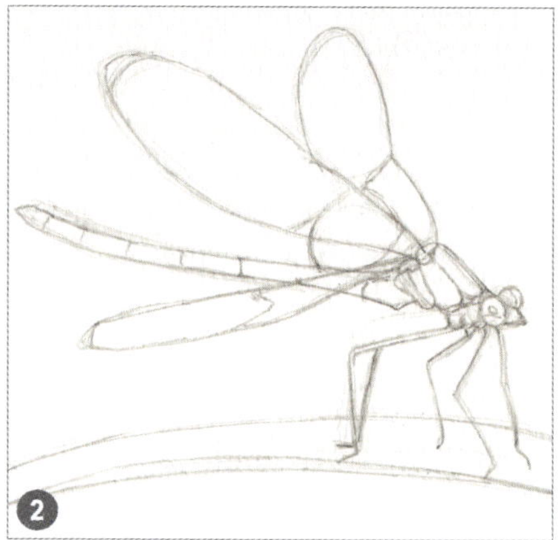

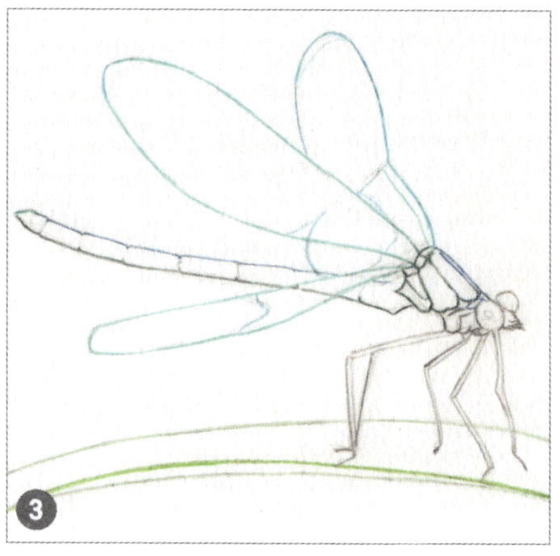

❶ Select your reference photo. If you are unable to take your own, many royalty-free image archives can be accessed online, including my own (see Resources). If you'd like to try taking your own, check out the tips on the previous page. I am using a bright and colourful damselfly image.

❷ Start with a graphite sketch. Position the body first, ensuring that the length of the body and wings combined are in proportion and fit comfortably on the page, with a good margin on all sides. Add a few details to delineate the main sections of the body, for example, or the position of the eyes.

❸ Use an eraser to "knock back" the pencil sketch until it is only just visible. You are now going to redraw your graphite outline in coloured pencil. Select an appropriate coloured pencil for each different part of the insect – make sure your coloured pencils are very sharp. Here, I chose various blues and greens for different parts of the body, and grey for the legs and head.

TIP:

When using a very sharp coloured pencil, try not to push too hard, especially at an angle, as this may snap off your newly sharpened lead. Use a medium pressure and hold the pencil more vertically.

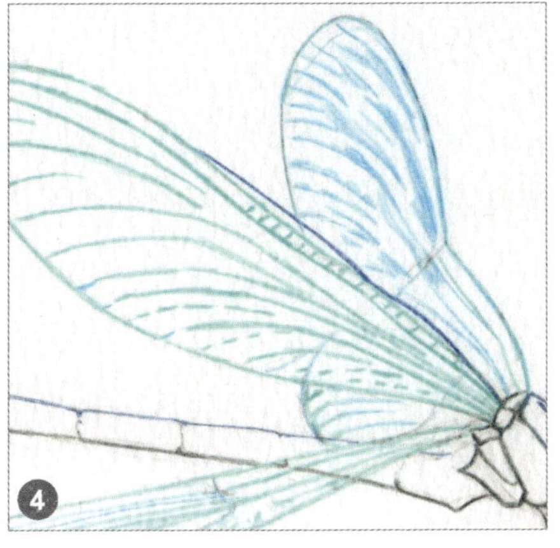

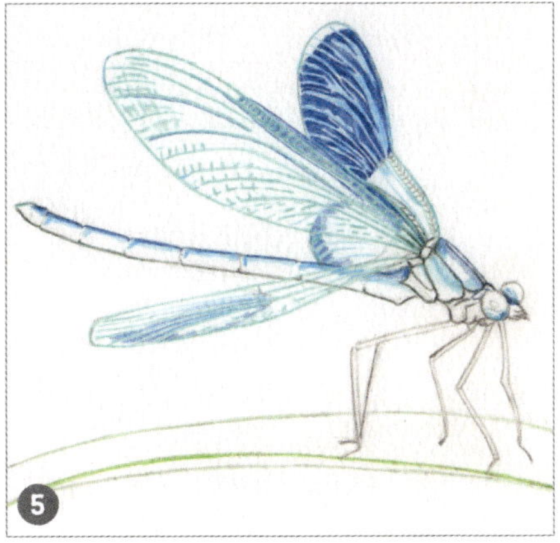

❹ Look very closely at the insect wings and fill out more details. I continued to use bright turquoise and green as I filled in these damselfly wings. Take your time with this step and use a very faint graphite outline guide first if you prefer, as this can be more easily rubbed out than the coloured pencil.

❺ Fill in around your sharp coloured pencil outlines; I used a phthalo blue and ultramarine. If you ever need to rub out some coloured pencil, a pointed or battery-operated eraser allows more targeted removal and is usually more effective for coloured pencils than a standard plastic eraser.

❻ Continue to add details. Look for one colour at a time across the whole insect and add it where necessary. In some places you will need to blend colours using the method described in the Introduction, Blending Colours. Find the brightest highlights, such as the sheen on the eyes, and leave these as white or remove colour with a pointed or battery-operated eraser.

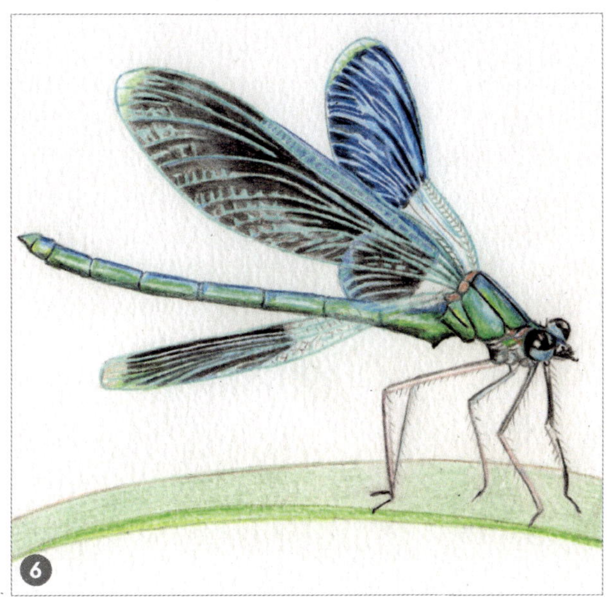

Gallery

It can be interesting to combine different types of insects from different river visits onto a single page. I kept a folder on my computer of all the insect photos I had taken, then when I was ready to create my insect page, chose a variety of water insects, flying insects, and times of year. When selecting your insects, think about the composition on the page, and perhaps vary the sizes of each sketch to make a pleasing spread – don't forget to leave room for notes such as species name and the date of observation, if you wish.

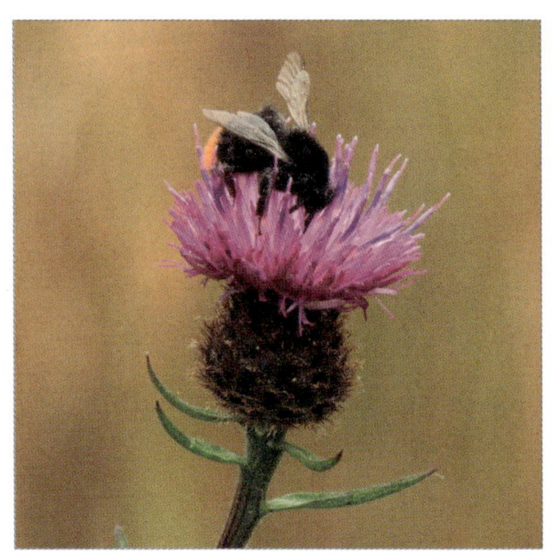

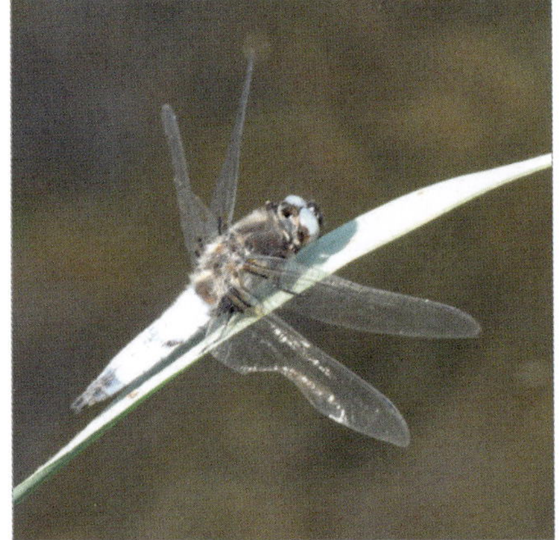

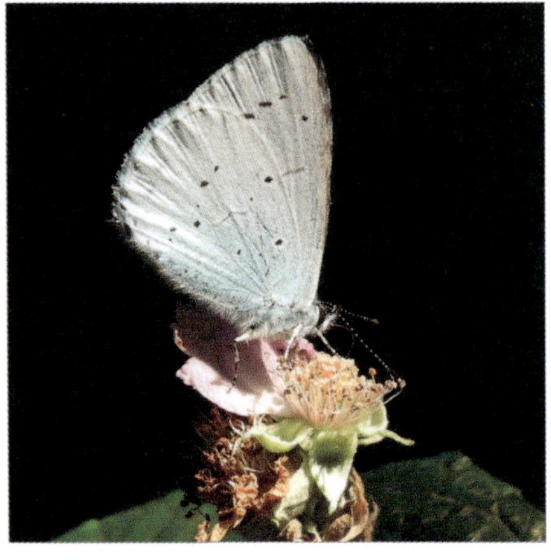

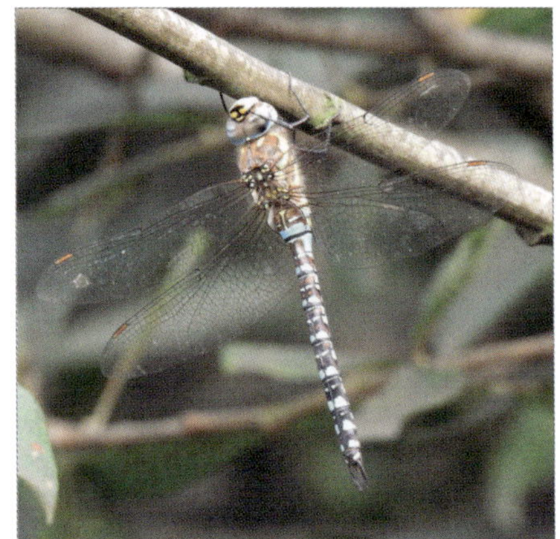

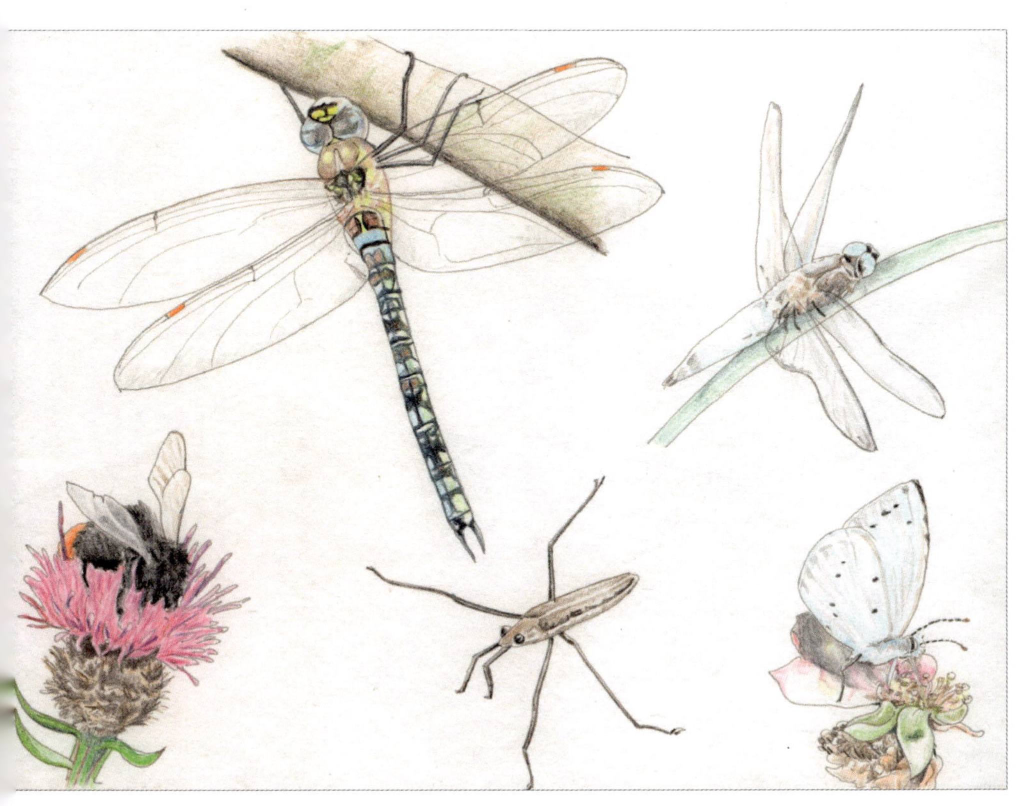

Lesson 12

Fish in Mixed Media

Fish are the main form of life to be found in the river, although they can be hard to spot and photograph. Usually, when we see fish, we will be looking at them through water, which creates an interesting challenge for the artist.

A mixed media approach can be a wonderful way to get around the difficulties of depicting solid objects through the shifting water surface. One solution is to use a liquid medium, such as watercolour, combined with drawing techniques. Watercolour creates a layer of fluid colour on which you can build coloured pencil detail, perfect for capturing a fleeting view.

For this exercise, a range of water-based media could be used, including bottled inks, ink brush pens, watercolours, or gouache. Make sure you are using a heavyweight paper suitable for watercolour, such as 200gsm (80lb) hot-press paper, or heavier. Your ink or paint will be used to form a base layer, giving all the advantages of a fluid medium. Once your water-based layer is dry, coloured pencil will then be laid over the top.

Additional materials:

Hot-press watercolour paper, watercolour paint, paintbrush, coloured ink or ink brush pens, white gel pen

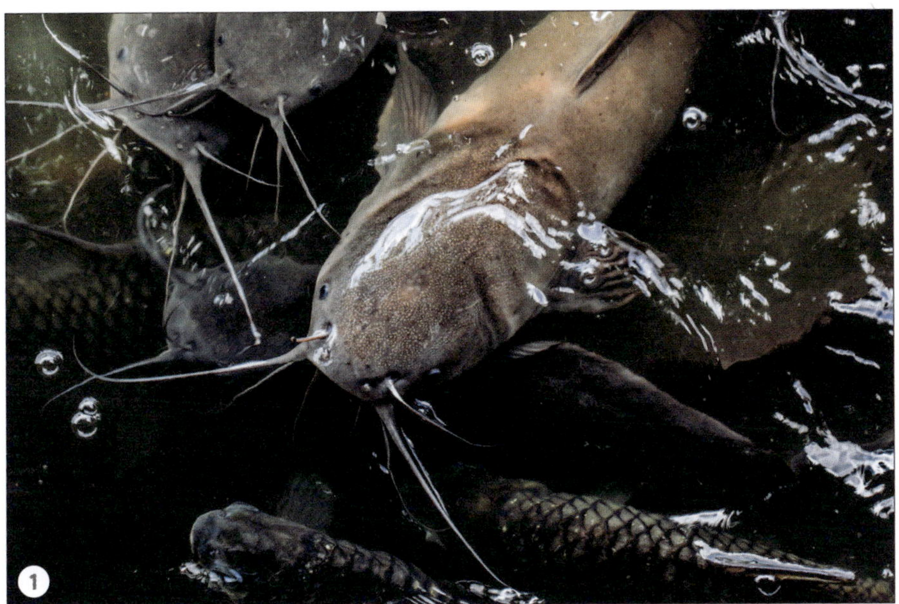

1

❶ Take or find a photo of fish just below the river surface. Some fish can be coaxed to the surface through feeding, while others naturally wait in the water. They are usually easier to spot in shallow streams or ponds. Photographs from fisheries could be used for this exercise.

❷ Start with a graphite sketch to map out the main parts of the image, editing the composition if necessary – remember you don't need to include everything. Here, I reduced the number of fish and slightly relocated them to space them out more pleasingly. If there are clear ripples or areas of light, outline these at this stage as you will need to leave them the colour of the paper.

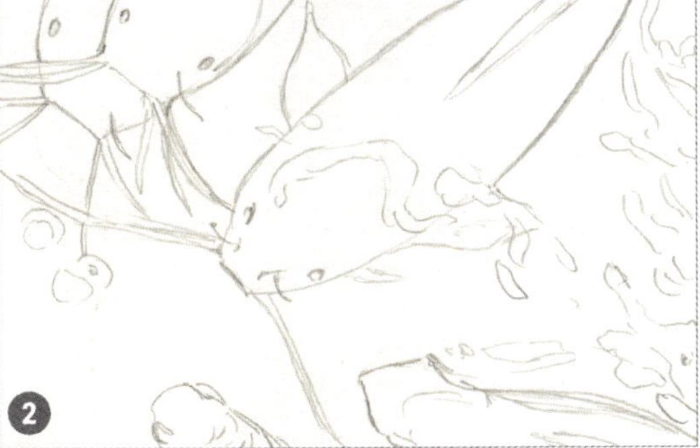

2

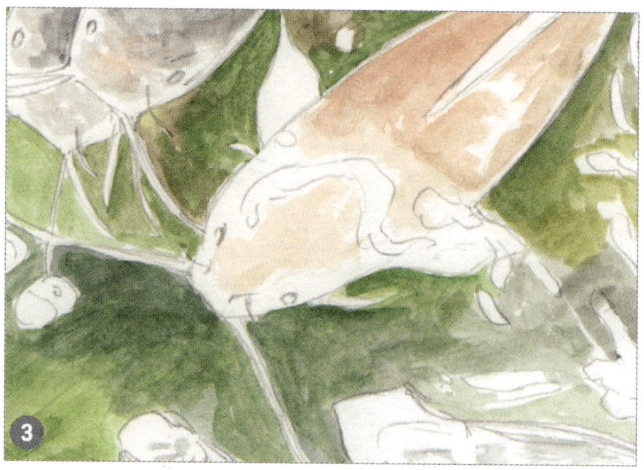

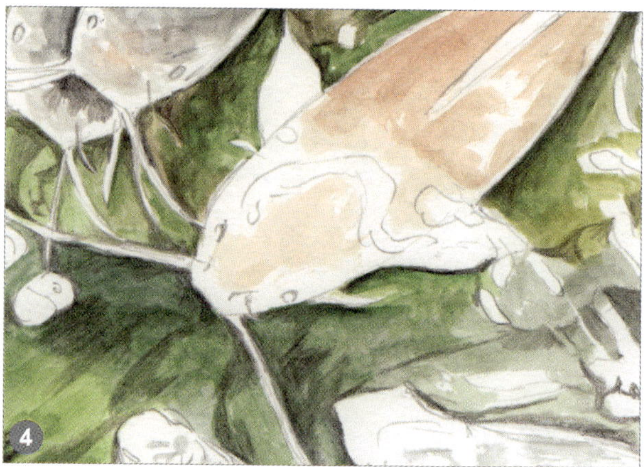

3 Now add your paint layer. There are two important things to try and achieve here. Firstly, try not to make this layer too dark; avoid blacks and very dark tones as you will be laying coloured pencil over the top, which needs to be visible. Secondly, now is the time to reap the benefits of the water-based medium, allowing the colours to blur and blend for the base layer. Avoid all areas you intend to leave as light-catching ripples. Allow this layer to fully dry.

4 Once the water-based layer is dry, get your coloured pencils ready and ensure they are sharp. Begin with the darkest areas, applying the coloured pencils directly over the water-based layer – try not to push so hard that the base layer is obscured. Instead, see if you can blend the two neatly, allowing parts of the underlayer to show through. Find the darkest areas and shade these in, using the benefit of your sharp pencils to delineate the fish bodies and major changes of colour more distinctly.

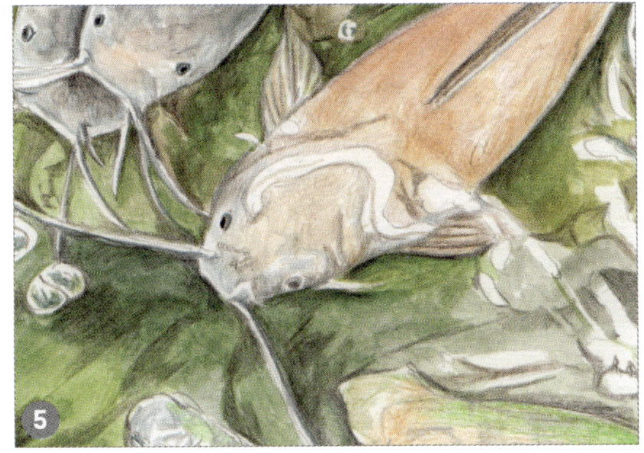

5 Use a wider range of colours to add more/further details. Working in coloured pencil on top of the water-based layer, increase the range of shades, allowing the base colour to show through the marks. Use scribbles and shading on the bodies to add form and build detail by defining the fins, eyes, and whiskers.

6 Continue to add detail until you are happy with the final image. If you need to add some highlights, such as the tendrils of the catfish whiskers here, trya white gel pen.

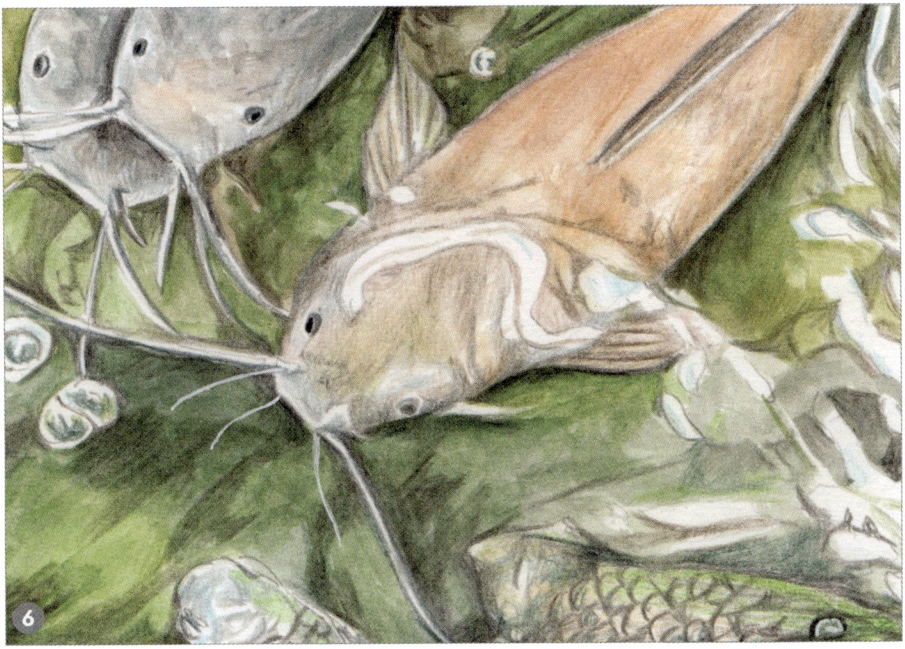

Gallery

This mixed media technique can be used even when there isn't a strong range of contrast in the reference image. In this photo of a brown trout from my local river, the fish blends in beautifully with the riverbed. I painted in many of the details in the ink layer (below), but then sharpened them further with the coloured pencil in the top layer (opposite). Notice that the colours have been made more vibrant than the reference photo to add interest.

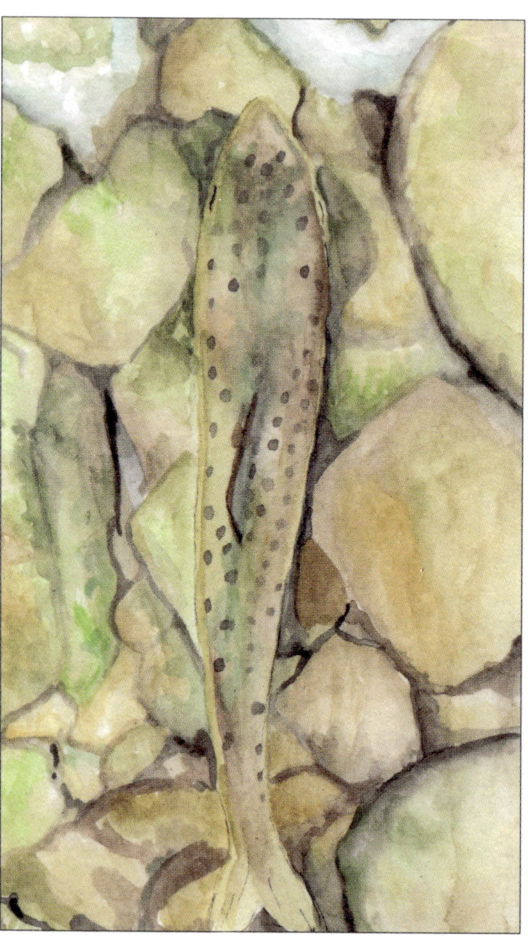

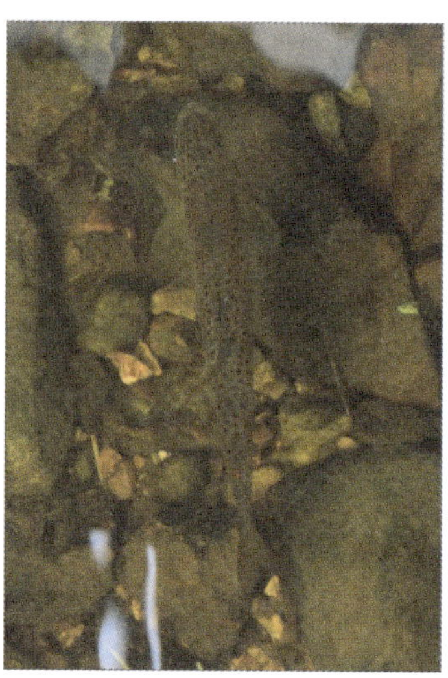

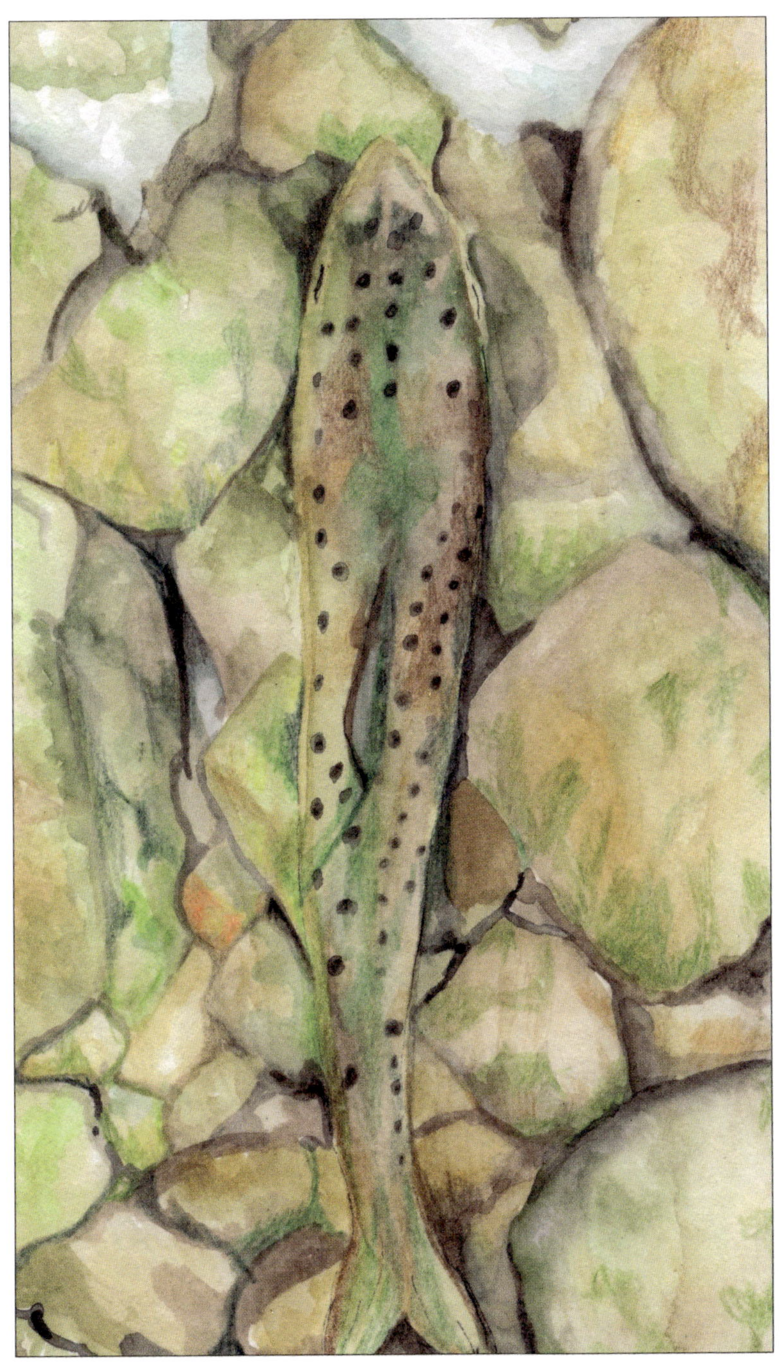

Chapter 4

Reimagining Rivers

By creating your river journal you will have gathered an amazing resource of information. In this chapter, you will be introduced to new ways to artistically represent this river data. Discover how mapping your river can highlight the features that have meaning for you, how to use artistic methods to display river monitoring data, use different media to extend your practice, and positive ways to raise awareness of the negative impacts of pollution.

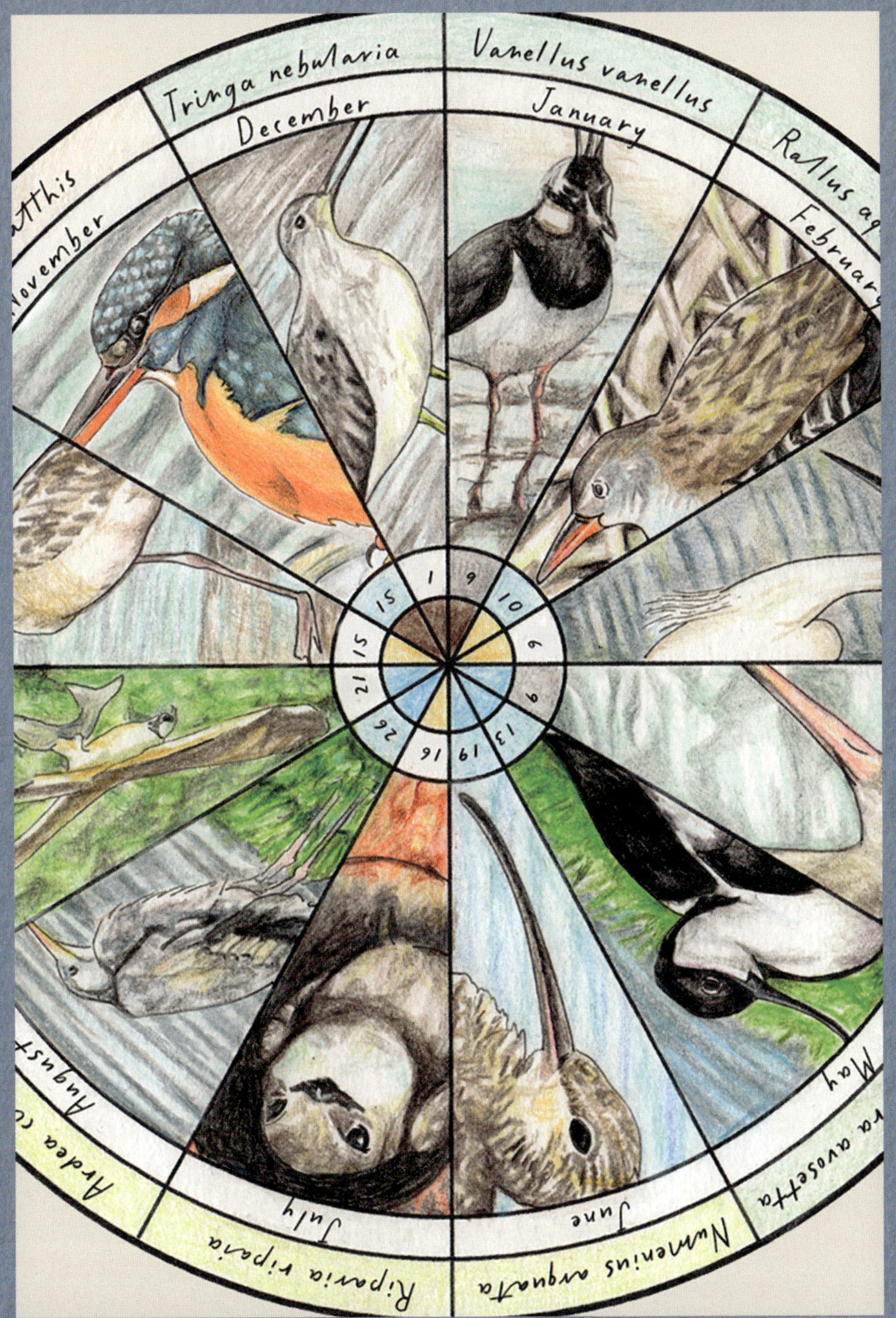

Tringa nebularia
December
Vanellus vanellus
January
May
Numenius arquata
June
Riparia riparia
July
August
1
9
10
6
9
13
19
16
26
21
15
15

Lesson 13

Map Your River

One of the oldest uses of artistic skills is the description of the natural environment through sketch maps. Using mapping techniques is an excellent way to get to know our river in more detail and can be done in ways that can have either a technical or an artistic style, depending on your preferences.

Maps are symbolic representations of places and don't need to be a perfect depiction of reality – they can include all the subjectivity that makes art enjoyable. That is, a map can be playful rather than rigorous and can be used to represent a memorable experience, such as a day walking beside a river.

In this exercise, I suggest three ideas for using maps to better know the river and express this information creatively. The first method involves making a walking map for the route you take when visiting your river. The second method is a creative use of satellite maps, and the third method combines nature observations with an overall map of the river.

A Walk Map

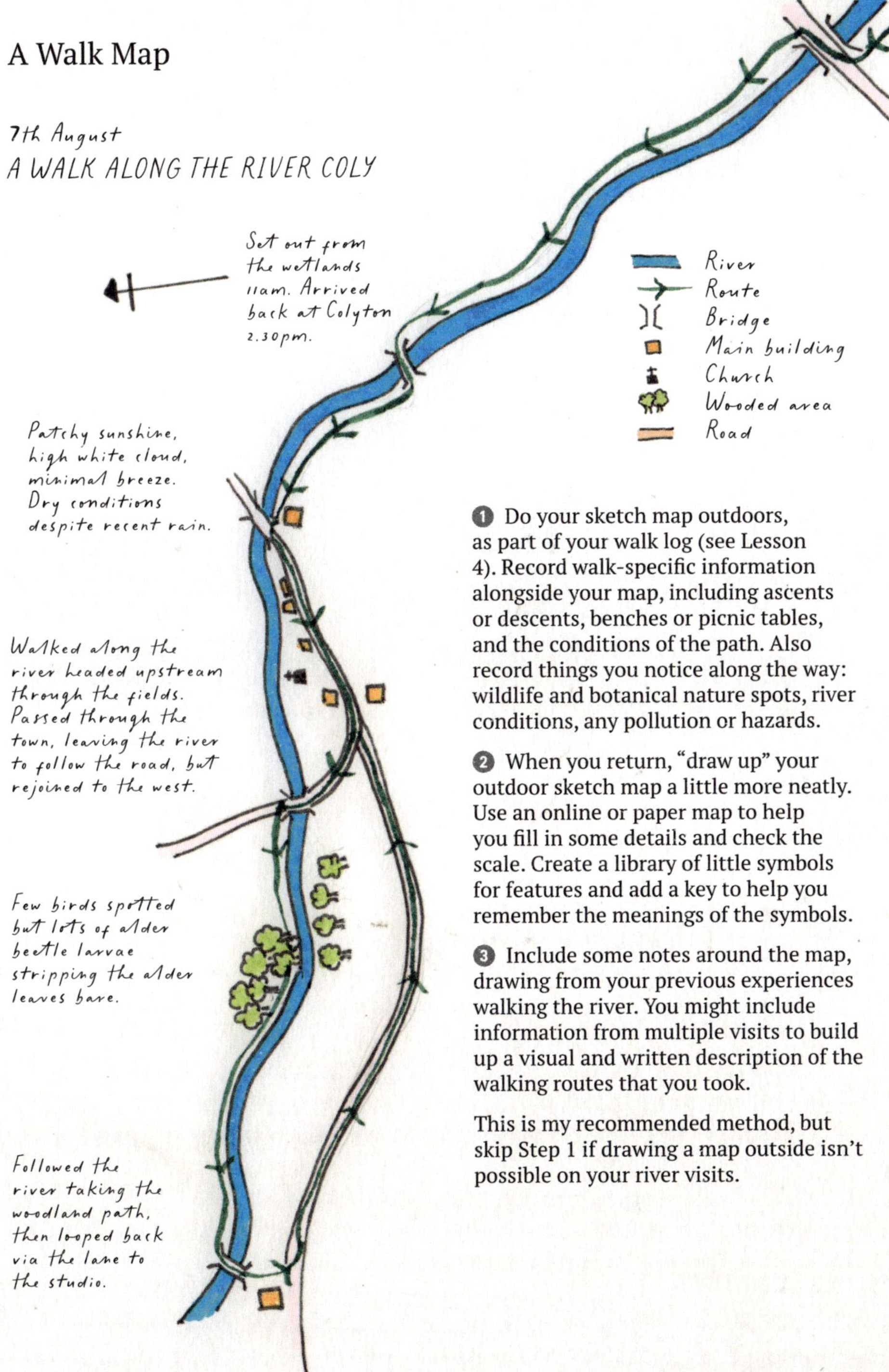

❶ Do your sketch map outdoors, as part of your walk log (see Lesson 4). Record walk-specific information alongside your map, including ascents or descents, benches or picnic tables, and the conditions of the path. Also record things you notice along the way: wildlife and botanical nature spots, river conditions, any pollution or hazards.

❷ When you return, "draw up" your outdoor sketch map a little more neatly. Use an online or paper map to help you fill in some details and check the scale. Create a library of little symbols for features and add a key to help you remember the meanings of the symbols.

❸ Include some notes around the map, drawing from your previous experiences walking the river. You might include information from multiple visits to build up a visual and written description of the walking routes that you took.

This is my recommended method, but skip Step 1 if drawing a map outside isn't possible on your river visits.

An Aerial or Satellite Map

We have access to some incredible resources online. Satellite mapping, such as Google Earth, allows us to get a look at our river from above and can be used to explore our river virtually, identify fascinating features, and as a reference for interesting drawings.

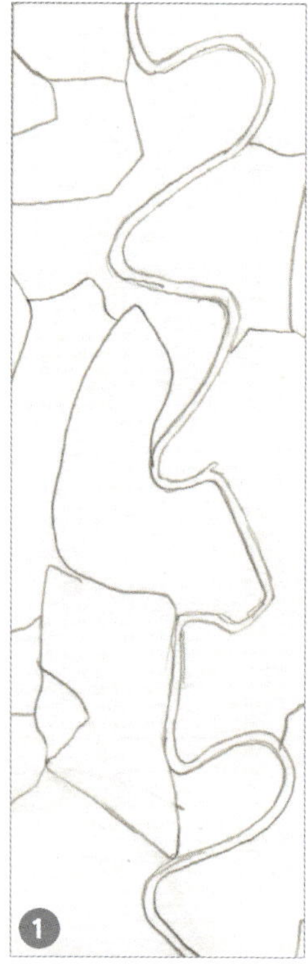

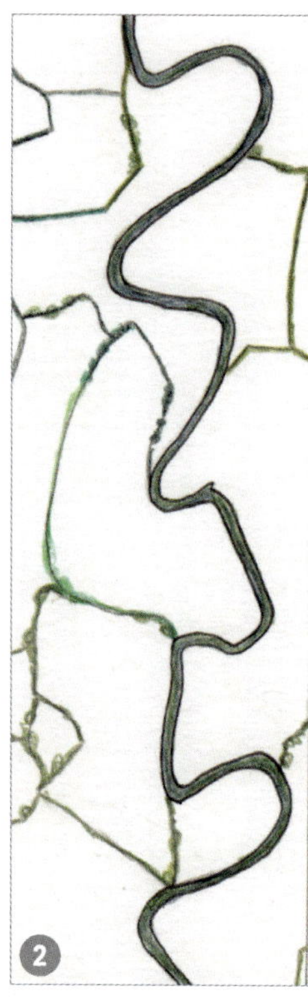

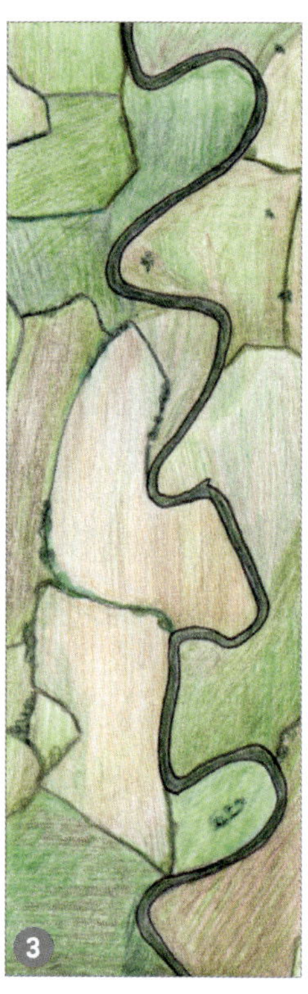

1 Draw out boxes; I chose a size of 17.5 x 5.5cm (7 x 2in) to use the drawings as bookmarks. Sketch an interesting section of the river. I included the outline of the surrounding fields, giving an abstract, patchwork effect.

2 To emphasise the river, use a black fineliner to outline it, then outline other major landscape features in coloured pencil. Erase any heavy graphite pencil marks.

3 Colour in the drawing using your preferred method. I used coloured pencil to recreate the interesting variation in the agricultural fields surrounding this river.

4 Track your river from estuary to source, looking for interesting sections. If you want to, you can become an armchair explorer and look at rivers all around the world. If you enjoy making these maps, use them to try out different media. I returned to the ink brush pens (see Lesson 8) to depict this river estuary, its organic shape making an interesting contrast to the rigid layout of the fields on its floodplain.

5 Look for areas of purely urban or purely natural land use along the river and see how they influence the shapes that you can identify. Sketching this area of equatorial rainforest was an interesting exercise in mark-making with ink brush pen and coloured pencil combined.

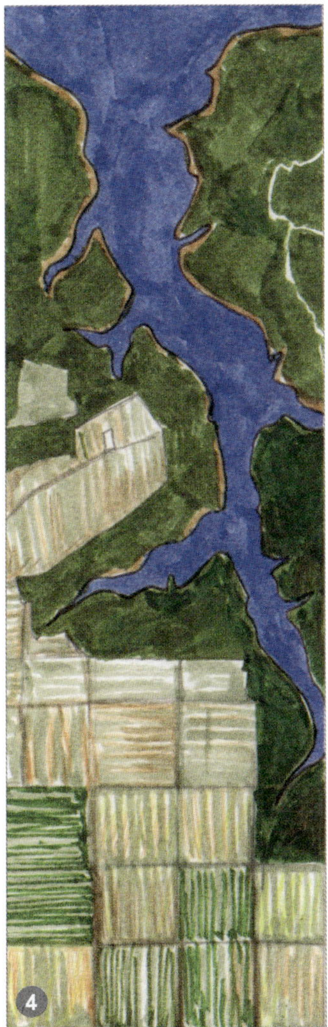

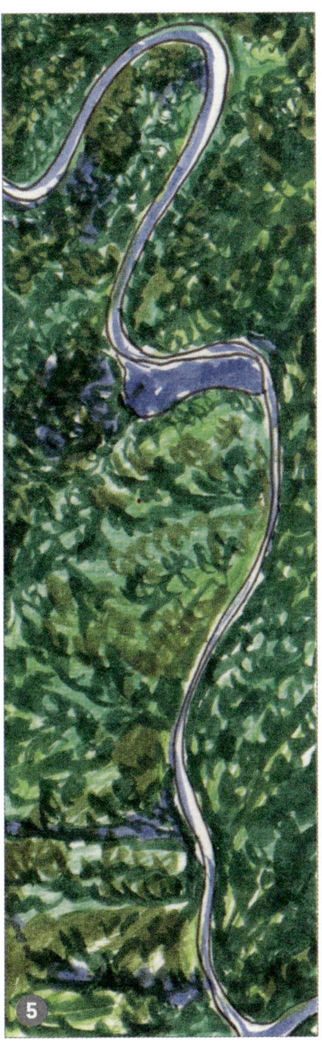

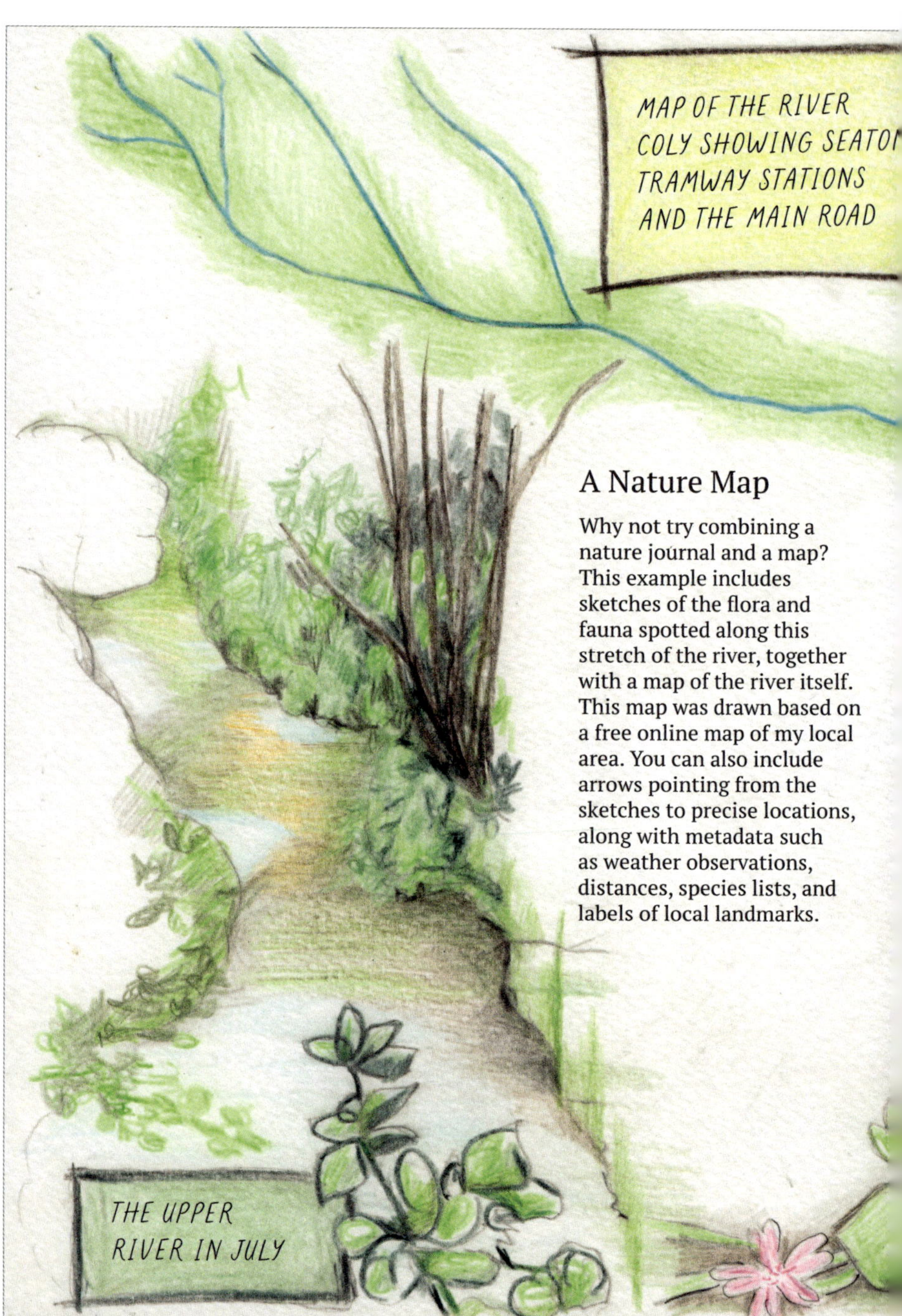

A Nature Map

Why not try combining a nature journal and a map? This example includes sketches of the flora and fauna spotted along this stretch of the river, together with a map of the river itself. This map was drawn based on a free online map of my local area. You can also include arrows pointing from the sketches to precise locations, along with metadata such as weather observations, distances, species lists, and labels of local landmarks.

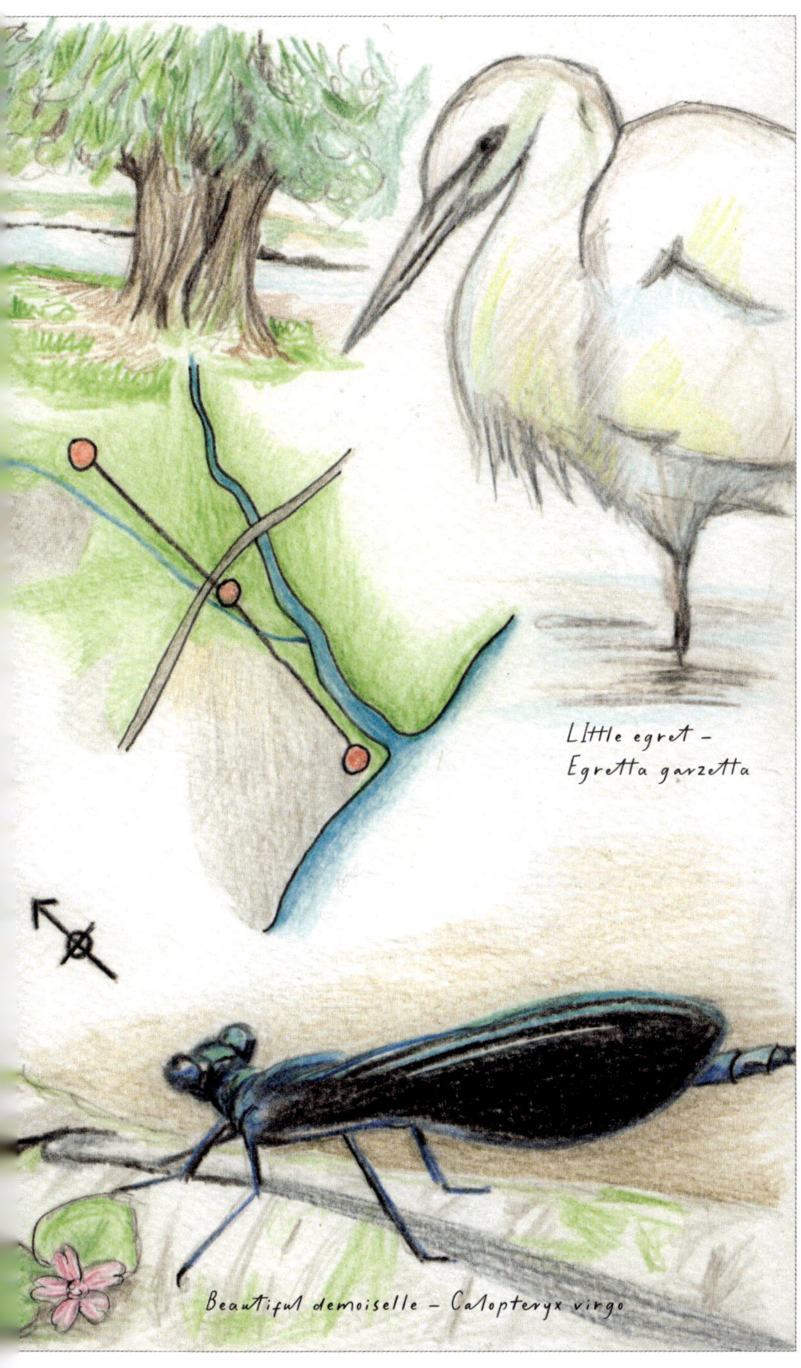
LIttle egret –
Egretta garzetta
Beautiful demoiselle – Calopteryx virgo

Lesson 14

A River Wheel

Phenology is the study of how seasonal and other cyclic changes affect living things in the natural environment. Phenology wheels are a visual representation of these changes and can be used to express visual, written, or numeric data creatively. In this exercise, we will adapt the concept of a phenology wheel to represent the river.

Many different things can be expressed in a phenology wheel. Often, they contain details of the weather, phases of the moon, tides, and plant observations. There are many fascinating river datasets that could be entered into your river wheel. The wheel itself can be annual (one segment per month for a year), monthly (one segment per day for a month), or follow a lunar calendar (one segment per moon stage).

The choices you make about how to fill the wheel will reflect your interests in the river so far. In my annual wheel, I decided to visit the river each day and fill the segment with a coloured pencil vignette of the water on that day. You might prefer to include nature observations or colour swatches instead.

Additional materials:

Phenology wheel template or ruler, compass, and protractor

1 Many free templates are available online by searching "phenology wheel template". To match those used here, there is a selection of annual (segments as months) and monthly (segments as days) printable templates of different sizes available at www.alexboonart.com. Alternatively, you could draw one yourself if you have a compass, protractor, and ruler to hand and a mathematical mind!

2 Decide how you will fill each of the areas in your wheel. Some of the smaller segments are better filled with a colour code or numbers. If using a colour code, be sure to decide what it will be ahead of time and draw up a key or reference chart to use with your wheel. If you're doing an annual wheel, write down the specific coloured pencils you are using so that you do not forget.

1

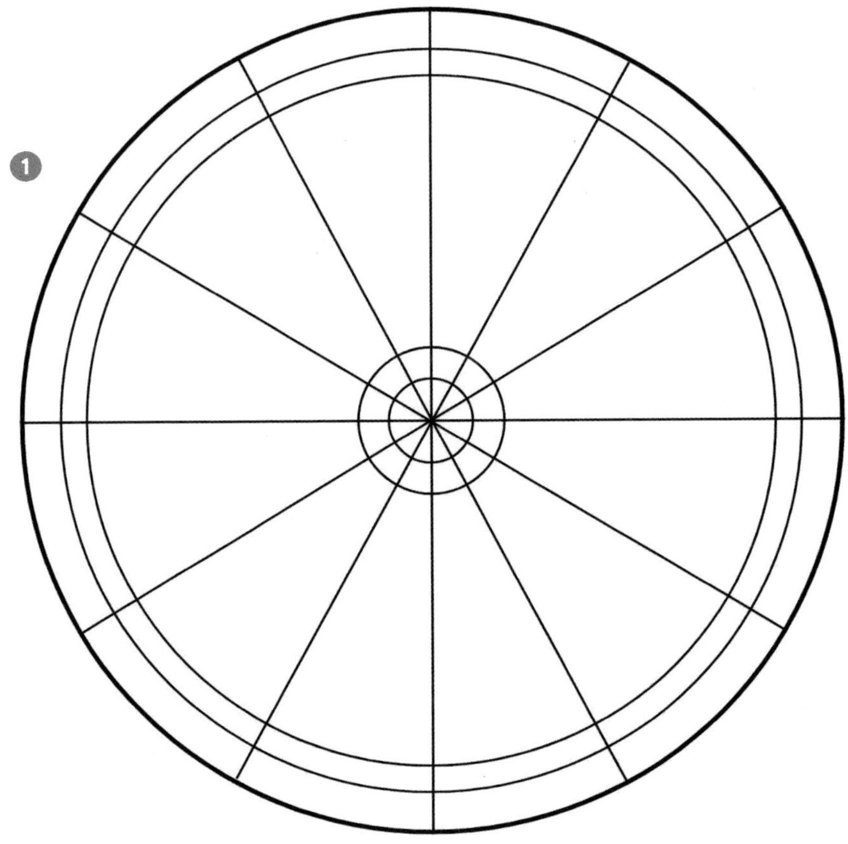

❸ Gather your data. Use gathering data for the wheel as an excellent excuse for a monthly river visit day out. You might go nature journaling and gathering photos for the other exercises in this book, too!

❹ Fill your wheel. You can either fill out the wheel promptly after each visit or wait until you have all your data and reference photos together and do the whole wheel at once.

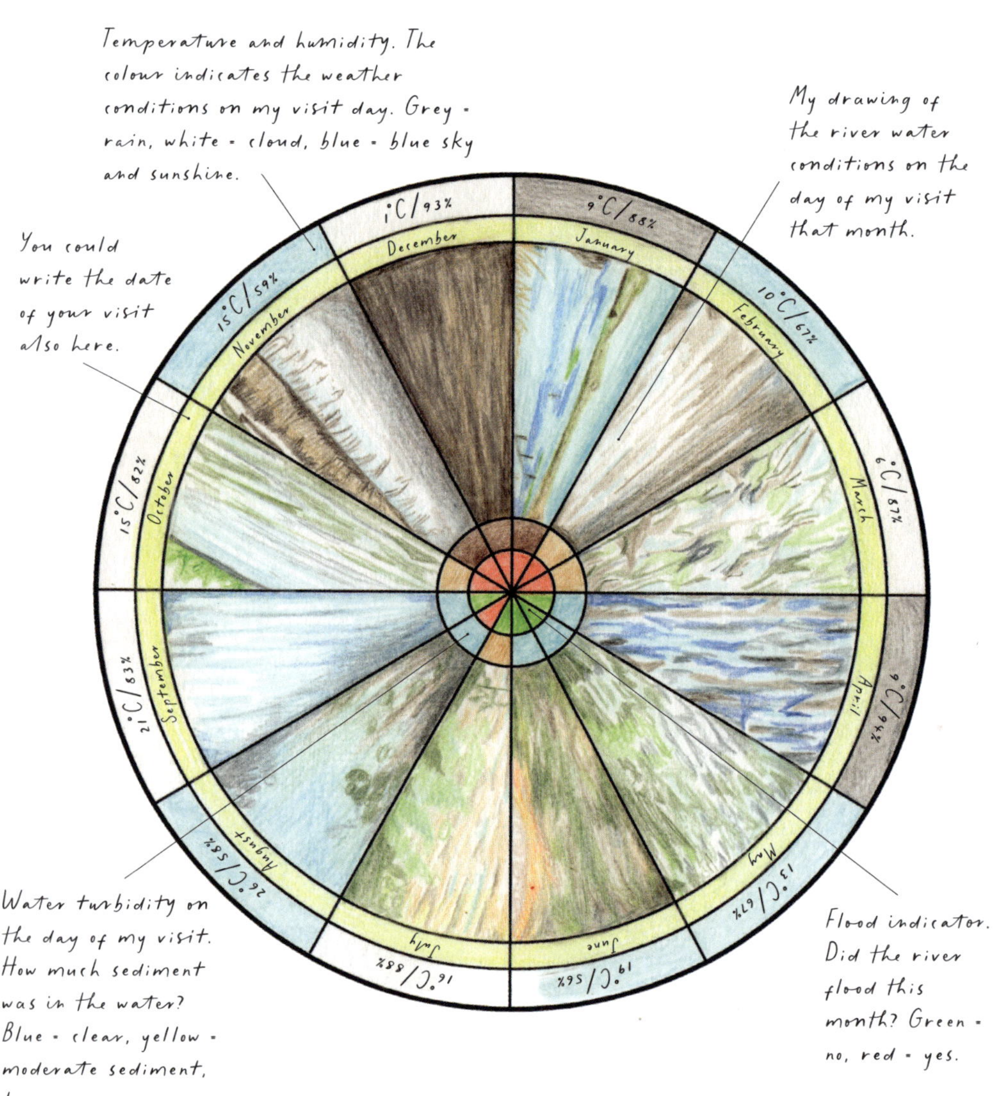

Ideas for Filling Your Wheel

There are all sorts of ways to fill in the river wheel. Try different combinations of the ideas below or invent your own.

- *Colour code ideas: Swatches to indicate river water colour or weather conditions, or a colour code for flooding or river levels.*
- *Numerical ideas: Collect data for general weather observations: ambient temperature, wind speed, humidity. If monitoring data are available for your river: pollutant concentrations, flow rate, river height, acidity, water temperature. If your river location is tidal: highest tide, lowest tide, tidal range.*
- *Symbol ideas: Weather symbols (for sun, clouds, rain, storms, snow, fog), river height indicators, symbols for different observed species.*
- *Drawing ideas: Quick landscape sketches of different parts of the river, a drawing of an observed plant, bird, or insect for each visit, a drawing of the same spot in every segment.*
- *Written ideas: Species lists, descriptions of the conditions, words to describe the weather.*

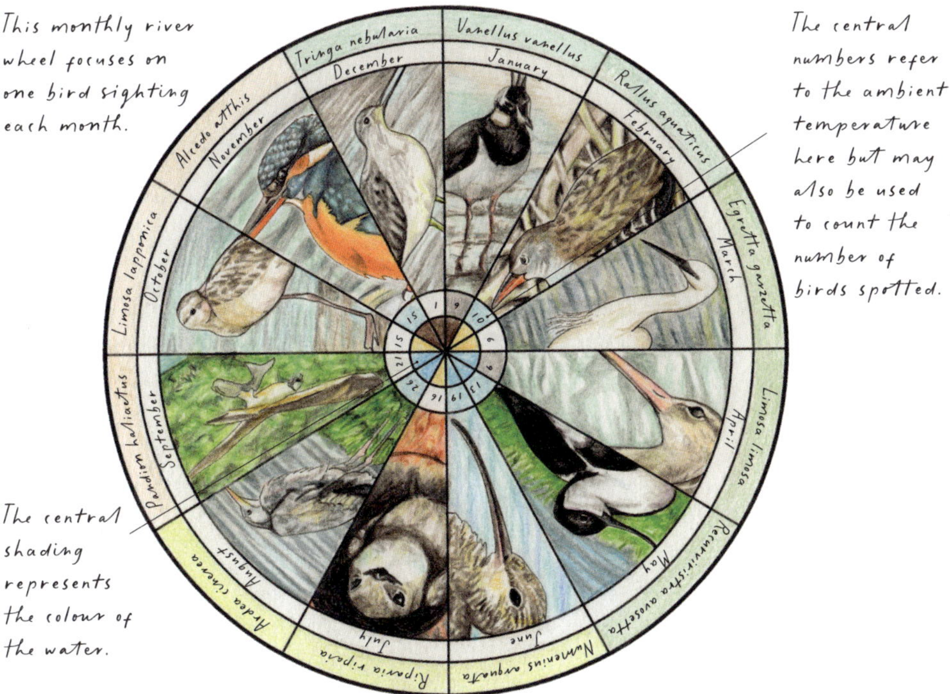

Gallery

This is a monthly wheel instead of an annual one, covering the month of July. Note that there is less room for detailed drawings in these monthly wheels, but since more frequent visits are needed to fill the wheel, the smaller amount of space is a blessing! The innermost circle is the flood code (green for no flooding, red for flooding). As I was focused on the estuary here, I included the highest and lowest tide and the moon phase in the next circle. The largest segment was used to indicate the water colour at the time of my visit. I used the same two-colour blending method described in the Introduction, Blending Colours. The outermost circle gives the day of the month and the colour code for weather conditions on that day.

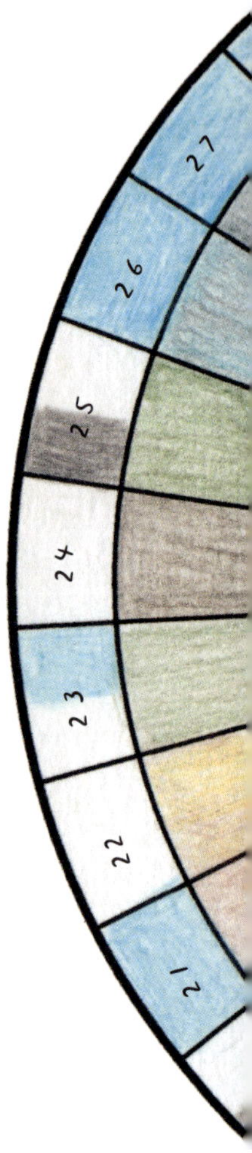

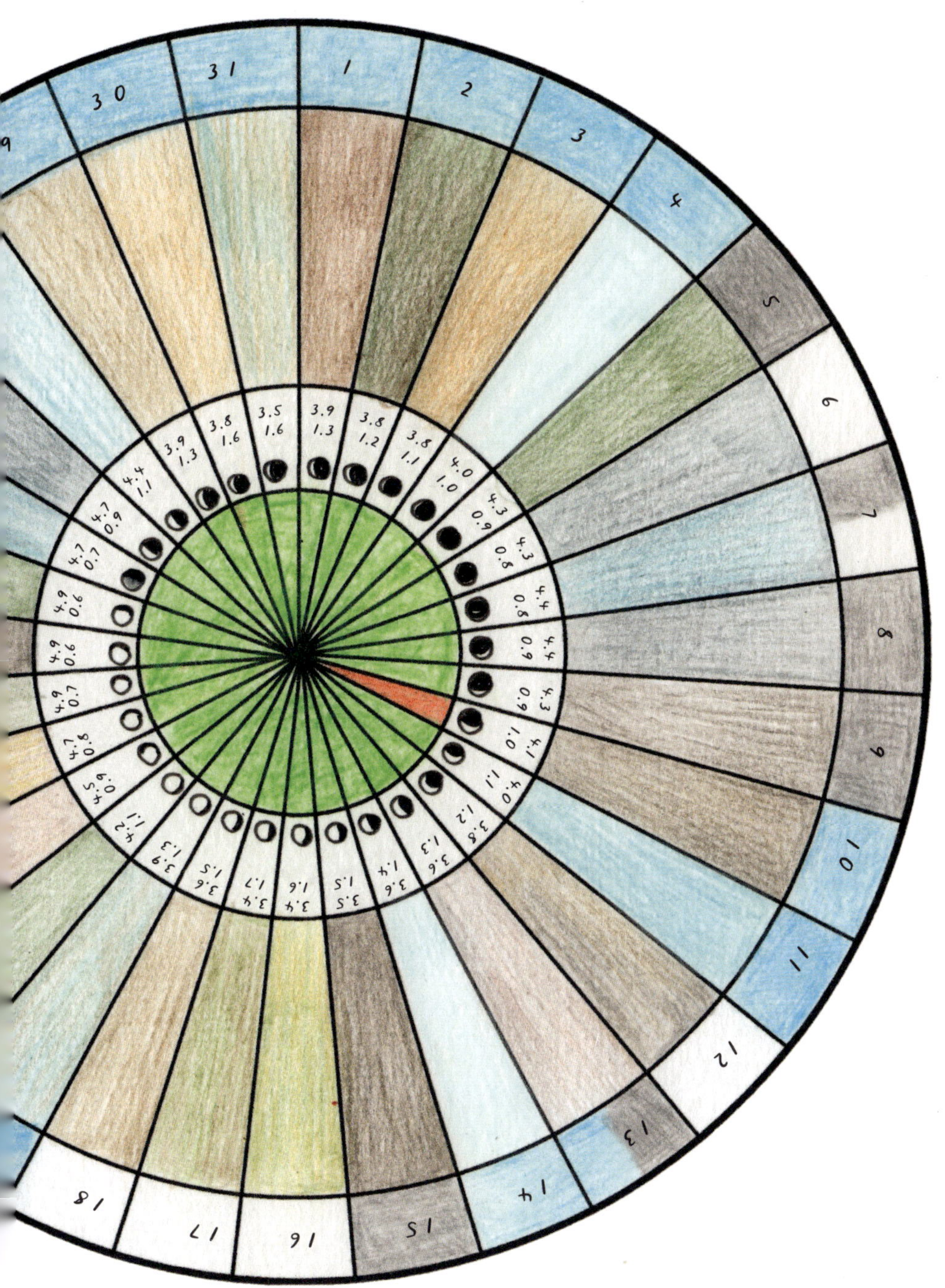

30
31
1
2
3
4
5
6
7
8
9
10
11
12
13
14
15
16
17
18
3.8 1.6
3.5 1.6
3.9 1.3
3.8 1.2
3.8 1.1
4.0 1.0
4.3 0.9
4.3 0.8
4.4 0.8
4.4 0.9
4.3 0.9
4.1 1.0
4.0 1.1
3.8 1.2
3.6 1.3
3.6 1.4
3.5 1.5
3.4 1.6
3.4 1.7
3.6 1.5
3.9 1.3
4.2 1.1
4.5 0.9
4.7 0.8
4.9 0.7
4.9 0.6
4.9 0.6
4.7 0.7
4.7 0.9
4.4 1.1
3.9 1.3

Lesson 15

Reflections on Toned Paper

Introducing different artistic media or styles into your repertoire will encourage you to look at your river in a new way. In this exercise you will use a toned paper to capture reflected light. The great benefit of working on a toned paper is the effect it has on whites and lighter-coloured pencils, which are often "lost" when working directly onto white paper.

The darker the tone of the paper, the stronger the effect on the lighter colours, and the less your darker pencils will show up. For this reason, I recommend working on a mid-toned paper so that you can work out in "either direction"– that is, going lighter than the paper tone and going darker. This is an interesting way to work in coloured pencil and can create unique effects that are particularly suited to "moody" landscapes.

For this exercise, we will return to the subject of Lesson 1, looking at still water, but this time we will render the reflections in coloured pencil on toned paper. Using toned paper gives the opportunity to really make the reflections stand out, particularly areas of white in the clouds.

Additional material:

Toned paper

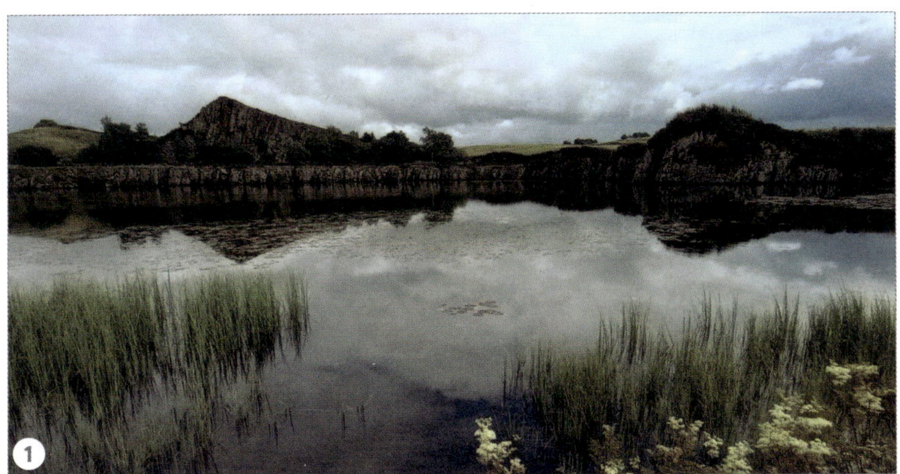

❶ First, choose your reference image. Lakes, ponds, or calm patches of your river are perfect as they will provide a good reflection on a bright day. Try to photograph your river or choose a reference image that has a clear reflection of the sky and/or bankside vegetation or features in the water. I selected an image of a quarry, taken on a bright sunny day with cloud present for interest.

❷ Select a mid-toned paper. A good range of paper tones are available, with the most popular being black, grey, tan, and occasionally dark blues or greens. I chose tan as a base, as both black and white stand out strongly against it, allowing me to work towards both light and dark.

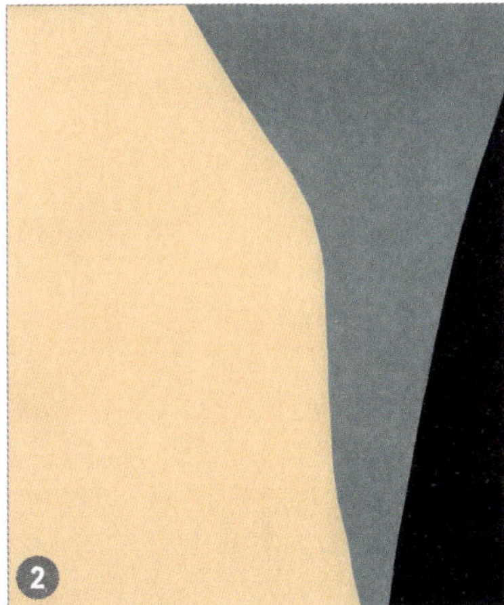

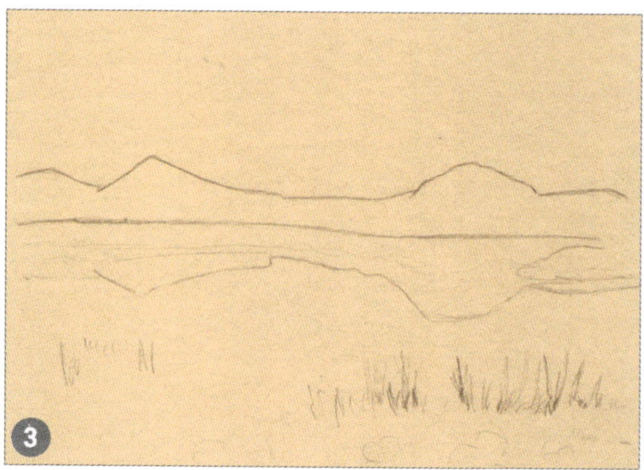

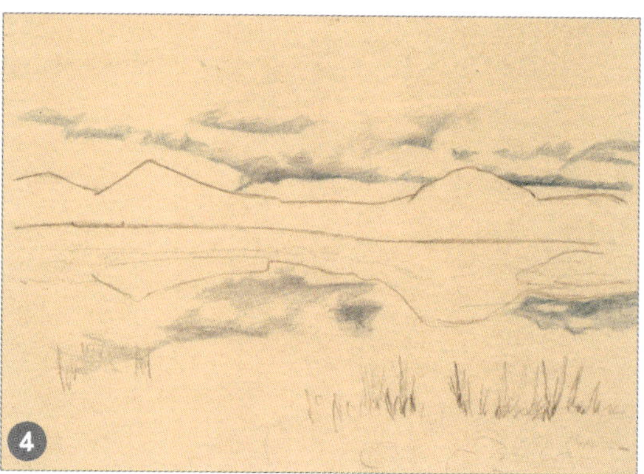

❸ Sketch out your scene using a coloured pencil rather than graphite. I used a burnt umber that was a similar warm tone to the paper. Remember that the decision of where to put your water/horizon line will affect your composition. You might choose to make more of the reflection by moving this line further up the page or make more of the sky by placing the line lower down. I chose to place the line fairly central in this example.

❹ Now look for areas of colour present in both the sky and its reflection. In this sketch, I noticed areas of dark stormy blue-grey in the clouds and placed these colours on the paper for both the sky and the reflection simultaneously. This saves time by switching pencils less often and also allows you to carefully examine whether you are achieving a good "mirror image" of each patch of colour.

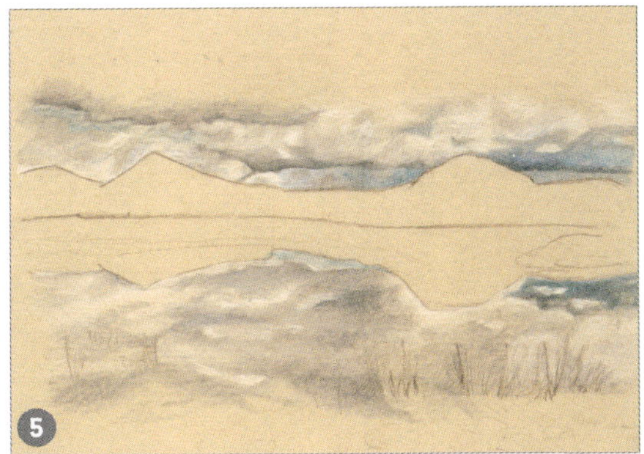

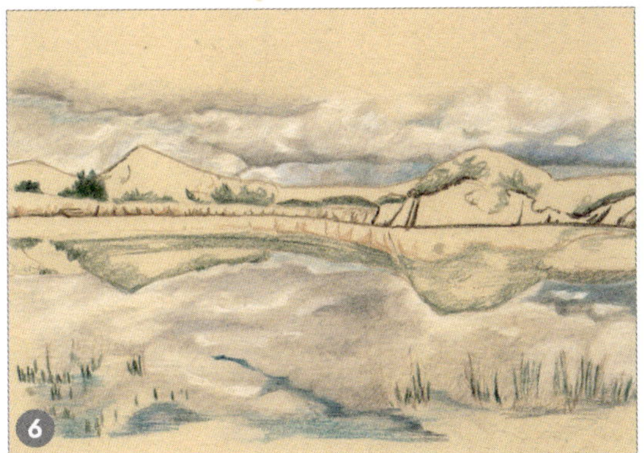

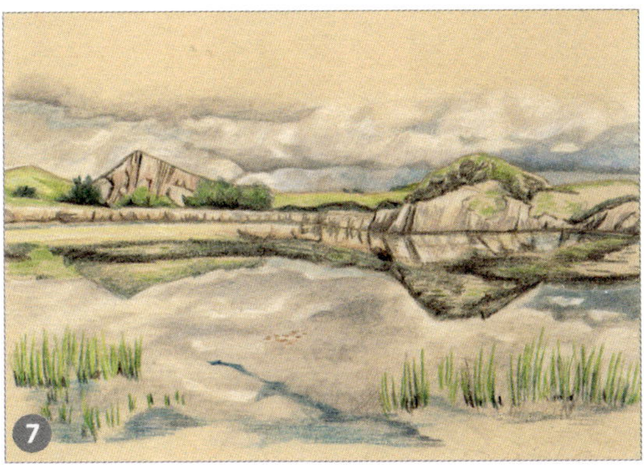

5 Fill out the rest of your sky block-by-block, immediately filling in the corresponding area of the reflection at the same time. Notice how the white pencil marks appear more vibrant against the base colour of the paper, and how the colour of the paper shows through the coloured pencil marks, giving the sky a certain mood. You can adjust how much the paper shows through by blending and using denser pencil.

6 Now work into any features or vegetation visible along the water's edge and immediately fill in the corresponding reflection in the water to ensure consistency of colour and position.

7 As you reach the later stages, look carefully at the reflection in the water. As discussed in Lesson 1, the reflection is very rarely a perfect mirror image of the objects on the bankside. It is often somewhat more indistinct, and this effect can be achieved by adding greater richness of colour and more detail to the features on the bankside rather than to their reflection.

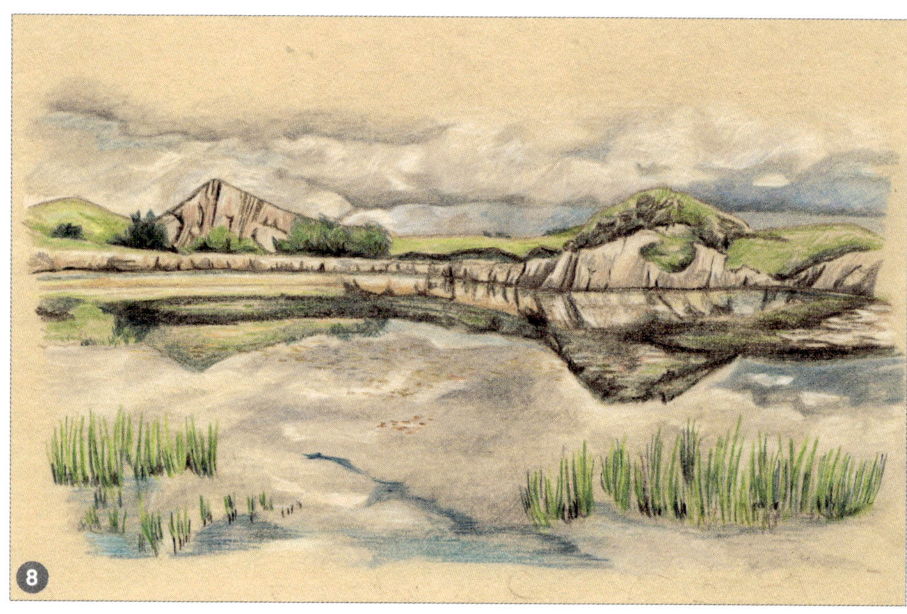

❽ To finish the image, look for ways to "break up" the reflection a little further. There may be slight ripples on the water or vegetation. In my reference image, there are reeds in the water and some floating algae or pondweed in the middle of the pond. Including these adds a further touch of realism to the scene.

Gallery

Using toned paper can also be very effective for larger-scale scenes without reflections. This sketch of a lake and mountain range was drawn on a dark-toned blue paper, which really makes the whites of the sky, snowy peaks, and lake "pop".

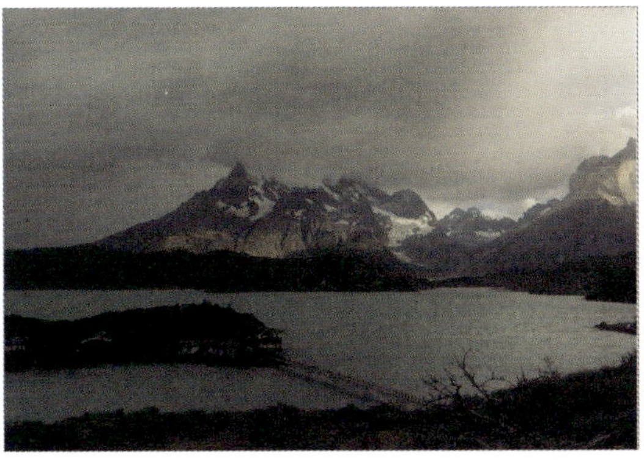

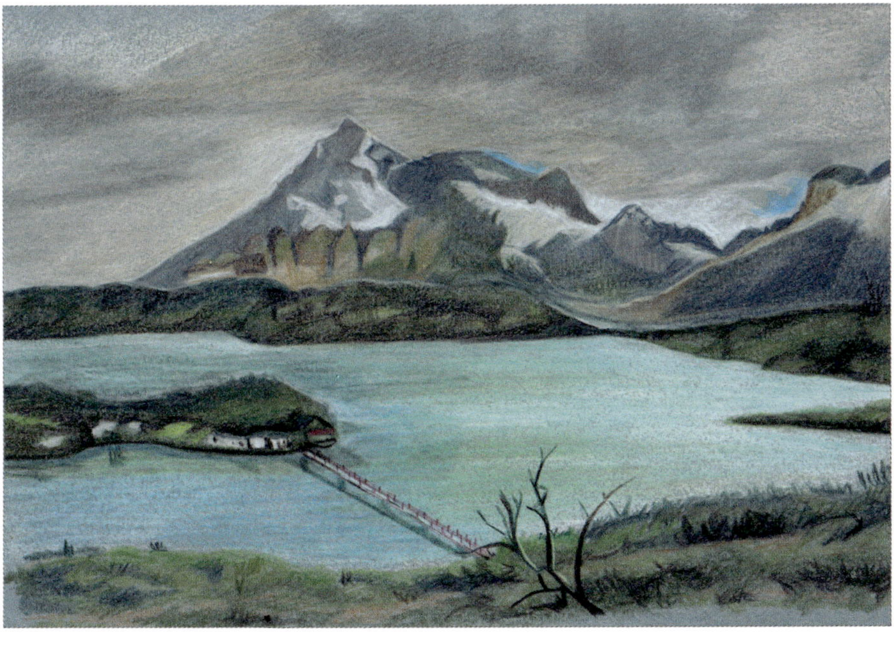

Lesson 16

River Pollution Collage

Pollution is a serious issue affecting most rivers worldwide. It may be a result of agricultural run-off, chemical waste from industry or mining, radioactive pollution, litter, sewage, or an excess of nutrients leading to high algal growth and loss of dissolved oxygen for fish. If we are being honest observers and reporters of the state of our local river, we must remove the rose-tinted glasses and also represent the less-than-beautiful.

However, a decision to convey the bleak and unpleasant needn't be boring or gloomy. For the last lesson in the book, we will use waste to bring awareness to litter and pollution of the waterways. This is an opportunity to be creative and have some fun, letting go of the idea of making a beautiful scene and instead having a play with colour and texture.

Much of the plastic that ends up in the sea originates on land and is transported after dumping in or near rivers. To represent this, we will create a collage using the type of plastic and packaging that would usually end up in the recycling or waste bin. Gather an exciting range of textures and colours to use in your artwork.

Additional materials:

Scissors, household waste, collage materials, EVA glue, paintbrush, paper tape

1 Find a reference image of pollution or litter from your local river to inspire you. If you have a very clean local river, cast your net wider to a local urban waterway or internet-sourced image. I found this reference image online of a river in much worse shape than my local patch. If you have a flair for the dramatic, you might do a beautiful river drawing of an untarnished scene and then add the collage on top.

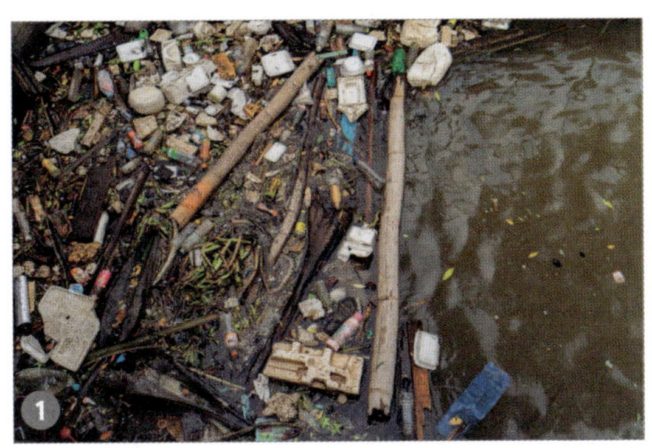

2 Gather your household waste materials over the course of a few weeks. When you would otherwise throw a material away, consider if it could be used to recreate the pollution in your reference image. Look for materials with different shapes, colours, and textures that can easily be cut up and glued down.

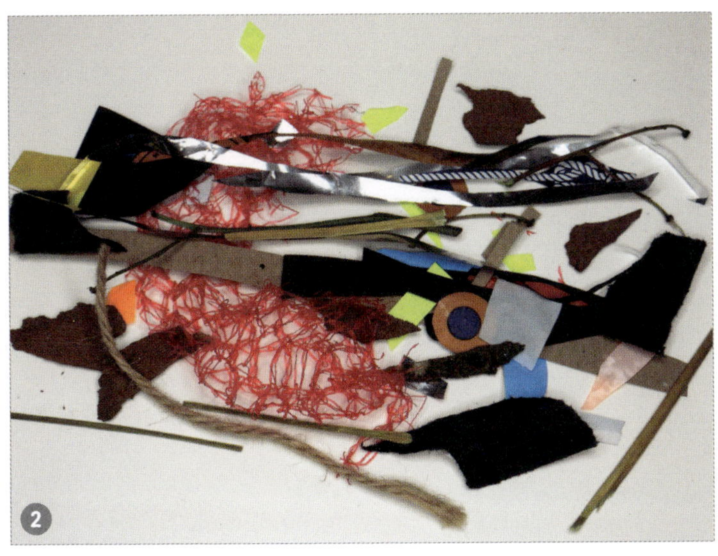

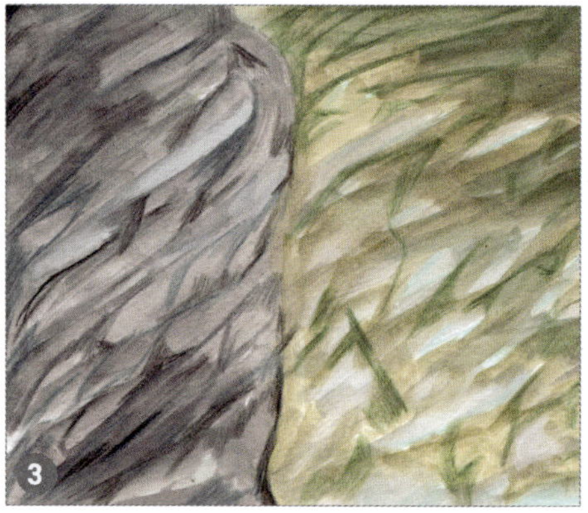

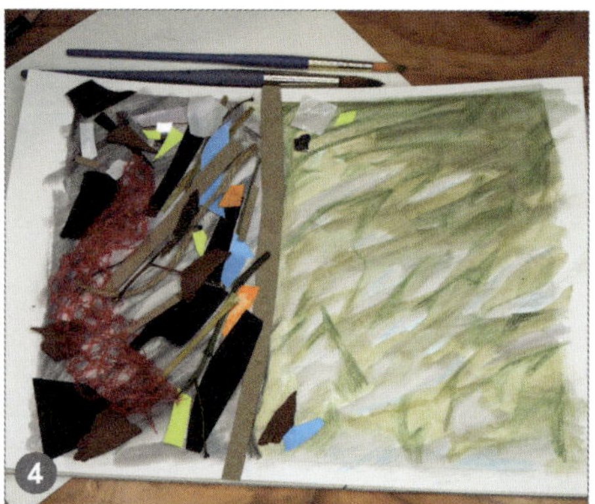

❸ Prepare a background for your collage. In this example, I used the same combined ink and coloured pencil technique as described in Lesson 12.

❹ Lay out a selection of your household waste materials over the background and experiment with different layouts. It may take a few attempts before you are happy with the positions. Take photographs of every layout attempt that you like and then use the photos to help you decide on a final idea.

❺ Fix the bottom layer of materials. I recommend EVA glue for collage as it flexes with the paper. Use a paintbrush to paint the glue onto the back of each piece of material on scrap paper before transferring to the picture. Paper tape can also be used for bulkier materials that are tricky to glue. You can either hide this tape or include it as a feature.

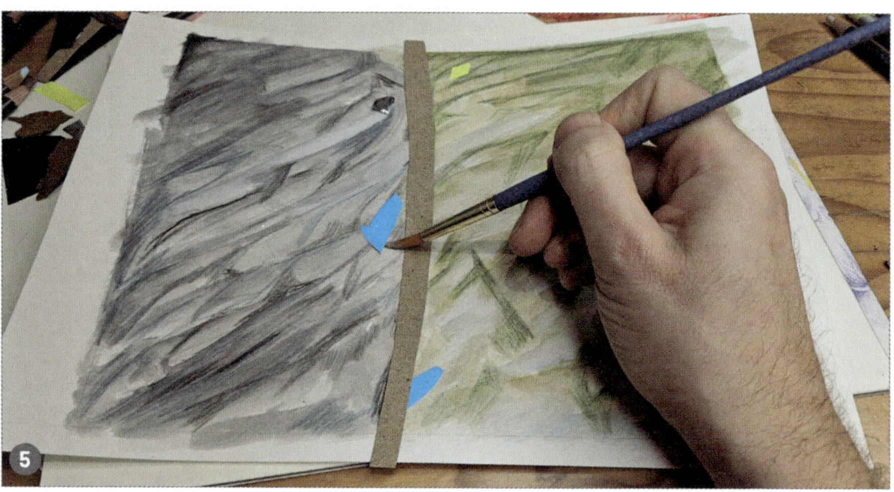

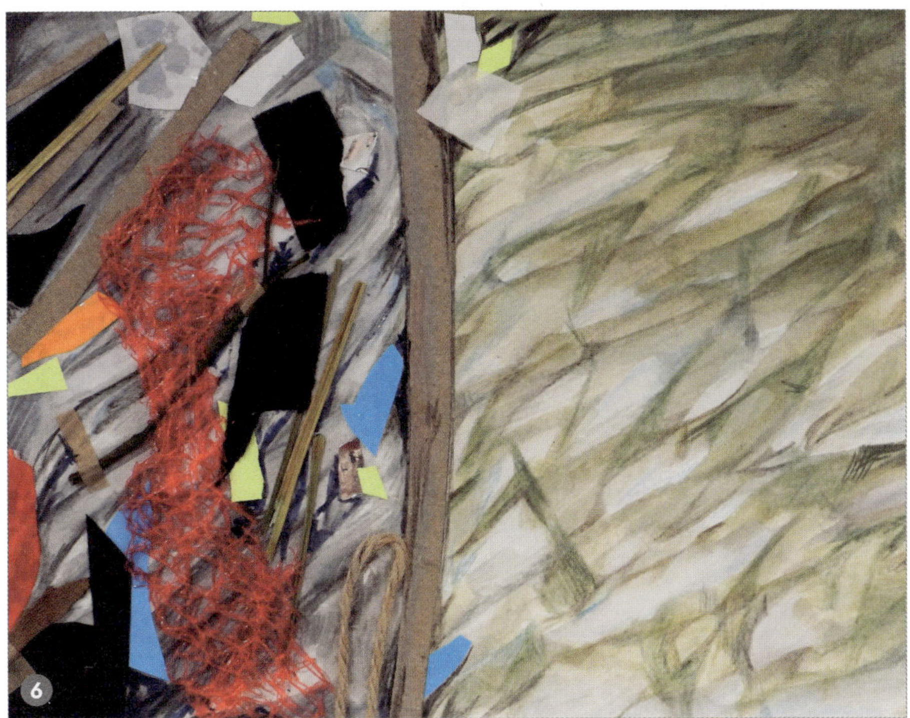

❻ Continue to add layers, letting the layers below dry before adding more. Once all the materials are in place, you can add some additional coloured pencil or ink marks between the items to suggest shadows. This exercise can be as realistic and serious as you want it to be – in my case, I just wanted to see how these materials would combine to make a generic polluted water scene.

Gallery

A less abstract example is shown here, in which I used strips cut from empty packets to embellish a scene of London. The underlying drawing was again created in coloured pencil and water-based ink. Rather than use the waste materials to indicate litter and pollution, I used them for reflections in the water and buoys.

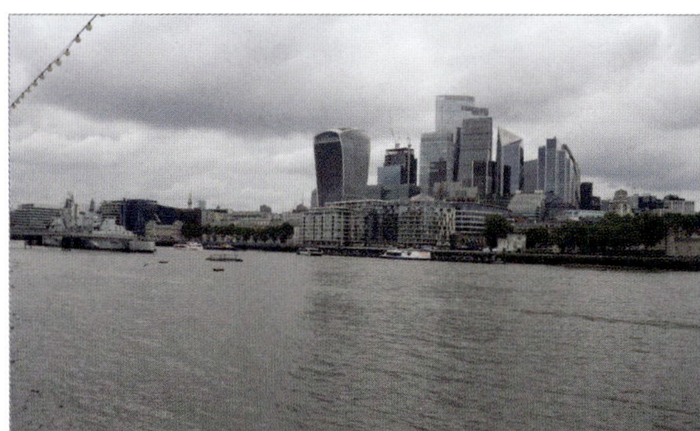

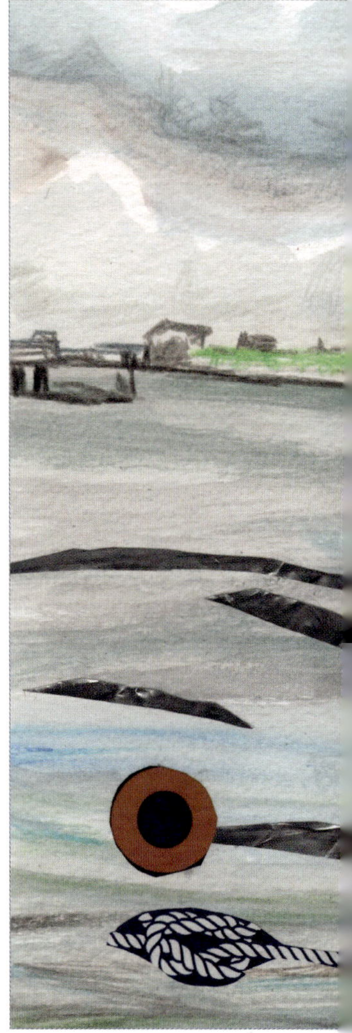

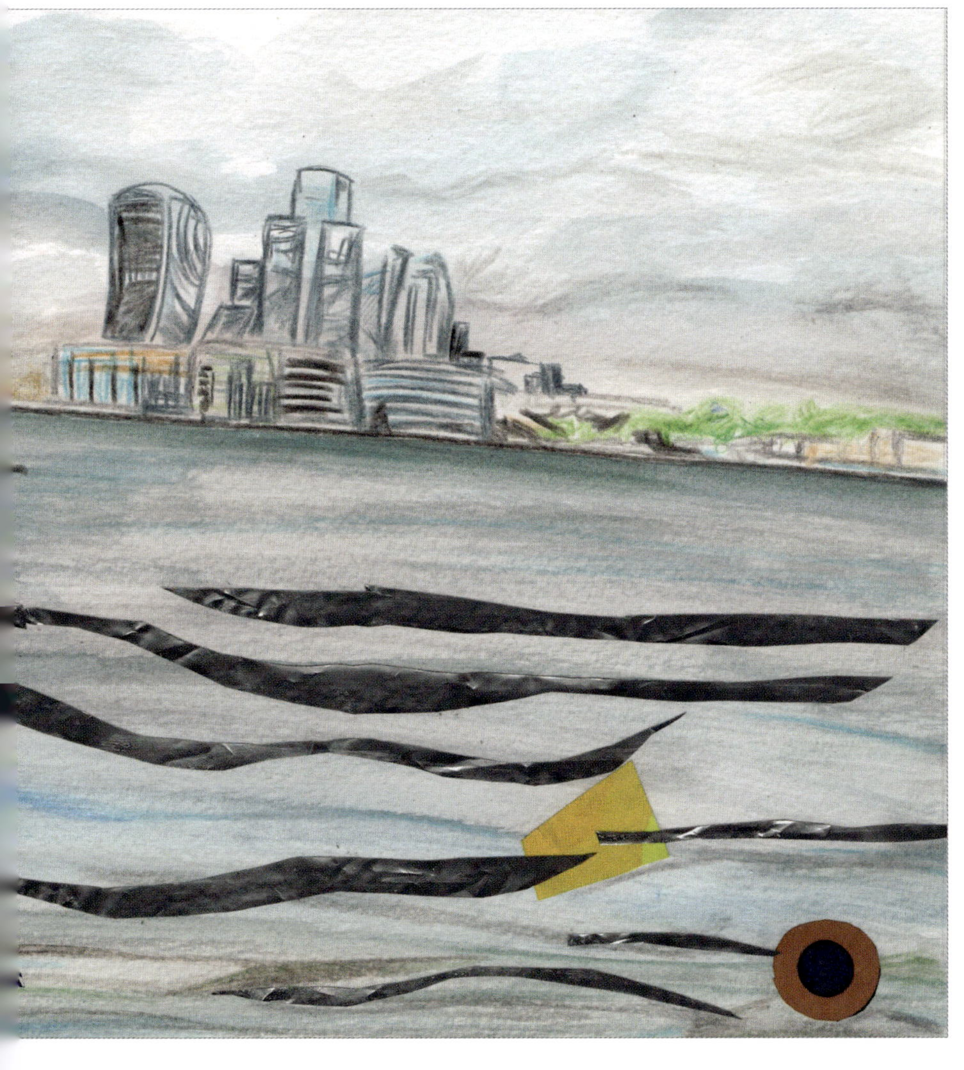

Nature Journaling

Nature journaling is the act of creatively recording your relationship with nature and can be an amazing way to get to know the natural world close to home. There are no rules about how to keep a nature journal, what it should look like, and what materials you might use. If you have enjoyed nature journaling the river, you might like to expand your river nature journal to cover more of your local area.

There are many ways to nature journal, but it is not always easy to fill that first blank page. Below I share three of my favourite prompts to help you start your first entry.

Meta Information

Always include the date, time, and your location as these are the things you will be interested in the most when you look back through your journal. Add a few observations about what the weather is doing right now, what the main features of the surrounding habitat are, and perhaps a few words about how you feel today too.

Prompt 1: What Else is Here?

Sit or stand in one location for at least 10 minutes. Close your eyes, open them, then write down the first thing you notice. Now ask "what else is here?" The things you notice do not all have to be visual; perhaps there is an interesting sound or smell. Keep listing as long as you can. This is a great way to find some things of interest that you would like to explore further in your nature journal or photograph and draw and/or identify back at home.

Prompt 2: A Whole-Landscape Diagram

Simplify the landscape in front of you into just a few lines. Perhaps the shape of the treetops, the horizon, points at which the vegetation changes. Now, within each section, list some observations. You might sketch a few plants from each zone or even write a paragraph about the habitat in each part of the landscape.

Prompt 3: The "Five Senses Plus" Method

Make notes in a location corresponding to each of your senses. You might need to be creative for "taste" unless you find something you're sure is edible. Pay particular attention to "touch" and "hearing" in contrast to the visual that we are in the habit of noting. There are so many creative ways to write out or sketch sounds such as birdsong. The "Plus" is your internal mood or feelings, which can colour experiences strongly. By recording these alongside the nature observations, we take that into account and place ourselves into the surroundings.

The Nature Journaling Circle

If you're interested in learning more about nature journaling and continuing to advance your artistic skills under my tuition, take a look at www.naturejournalingcircle.com. This online art school and community provides:

- *Courses and tutorials on nature journaling and art techniques.*
- *Monthly live tutorial and social chats via Zoom.*
- *A growing on-demand library of all past tutorial content.*
- *Motivation to keep journaling, with templates, resources, and monthly prompts.*
- *A friendly journal-sharing community forum.*

Join in with a monthly or annual membership, by purchasing an on-demand course, or by joining the community sharing space for free. We would love to see your creations inspired by the lessons in this book!

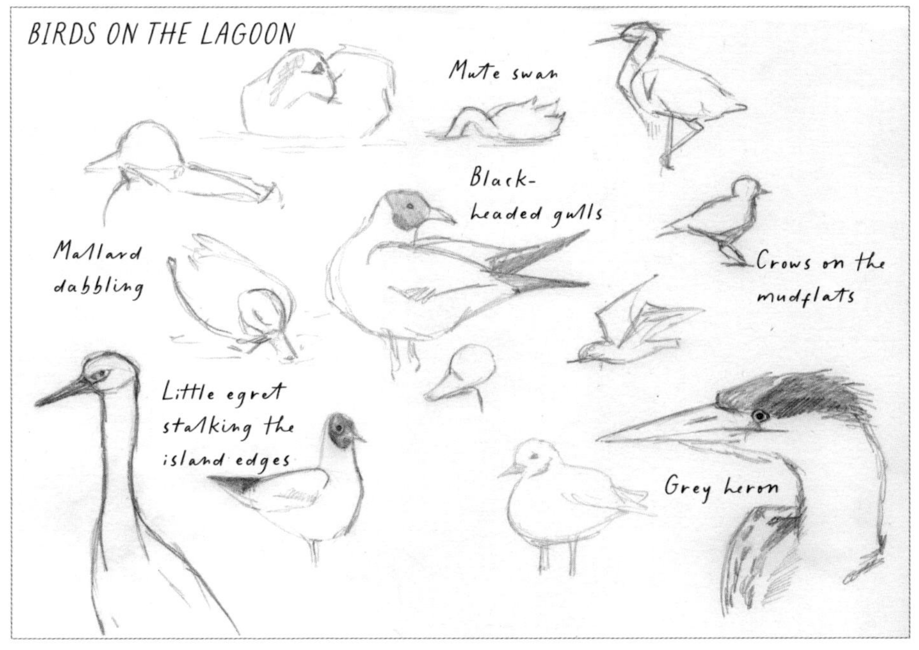

Identifying Species

Over the years, I have developed a creativity-forward process for reaching a species identification. This method is designed to be slow and thoughtful, with the intention of mindful learning rather than reaching a quick answer. Use this method as often as you can, and you will find that the species names will stay with you for longer. You can add these notes to your nature journal, or create a separate species field book of your own.

Step 1: Sketch, Sample, and Photograph

First, gather as much information as you can in the field. Look for the most distinguishing features of any given species. For a river bird this might be body shape, type of beak, eye position, and what the legs and feet look like. Observe behaviours, particularly feeding. Note whether there are similar birds close by or whether this individual is isolated. Describe the features of the habitat – which part of the river are you on? You can use a similar sketching and questioning approach for other types of organism, such as river insects, or any local flora, such as rushes or reeds. Take plenty of photographs.

Step 2: Use a Guidebook

A good field guide is a fantastic resource. There are thousands of localised and subject-specific guidebooks available, so here are a few tips on finding a good reference book:

- Choose a relatively recent edition as species names can change; more recent editions often include changes in distribution as a result of climate change or biodiversity losses.
- Check that the guidebook is suitable for your region; often a more localised book is more useful than a general guide to global or continental species.
- The choice between photos or illustrations is a matter of personal preference. Illustrations are often better as they isolate important features, although photos may allow for a more immediate comparison.
- To study a river, you may need several different guidebooks, such as one for river and sea birds, one for aquatic insects, another for fish, another for water plants, and so on. Be aware that most guidebooks are limited in scope and wider research may be needed.

Step 3: Internet and Apps

Identification apps can be incredibly helpful in our search for a species identification and will result in a quick answer. However, as responses are immediate, the temptation is for this to be the only stage in the identification process. Try not to let this happen, at least not all the time. See the Resources section for a few app suggestions.

The internet is another useful resource. Image searches can be used to compare similar species with your records, or to obtain further photographs based on a guess from a guidebook. Sometimes, typing a list of keywords such as "small wading bird, red beak, red legs, river estuary, UK" into a search engine can produce useful websites to help narrow down your search.

Step 4: Got Your Result? Don't Stop There!

Knowing the species name is only the first step in getting to know a species. Guidebooks and internet searches open up worlds of information. Archival, herbal, foraging, and folk histories are just as interesting as scientific data. Get stuck in: perhaps you can use this extra information to annotate your sketches.

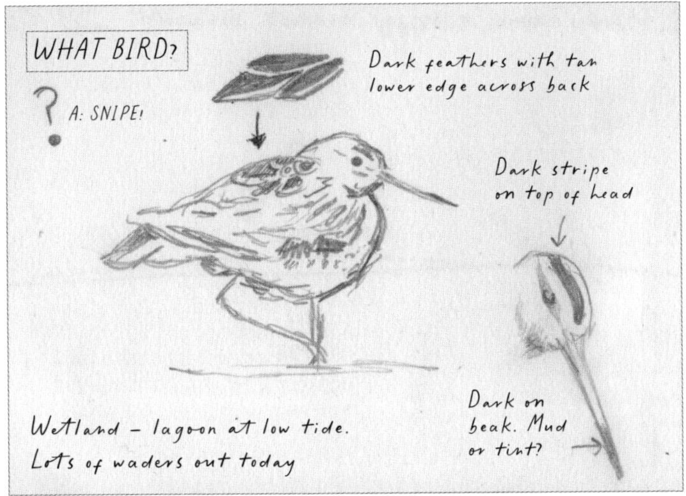

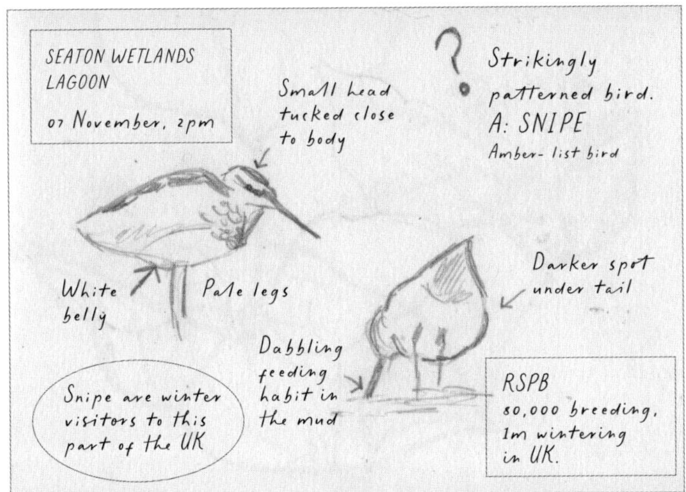

TIP:

Scribble down a big question mark or ask a question such as "What bird?" in your journal, perhaps in a different colour. This will remind you to answer the question later.

Art in Stewardship

Creativity in nature can do so much for our wellbeing and it also develops a feeling of love and care for the locations that we observe in detail. Love grows from intimate knowledge of a species or place, and we naturally want to protect the things that we love.

Rivers worldwide are in peril, with pressures such as pollution and overdevelopment. You might have even noticed some of these pressures on your own local stretch and wondered how you can help. Just as a life-drawing artist will pay their sitter, how can we repay our river for all the inspiration it has given us through this project? Below are a few ideas from my own experiences with river stewardship, but be creative and ask around – there may be some other way you can help.

Volunteer

River monitoring projects are springing up all over the world, particularly in areas that lack funding for official national monitoring. See if your river has a group of volunteers and observers dedicated to tracking its health that you can join. If not, if you have the time and skills to offer, you might help begin one of these vital community groups.

Donate

If you cannot donate your time, perhaps consider a regular donation to a river-focused charity. There are also charities and organisations focused on conservation of specific river environments such as wetlands, source bogs, and mangroves. Many charities circulate wonderful educational materials and newsletters to their members and may have events that you can join online or in person.

Inspire Others

One of the ultimate ways to give back is to inspire the same love for nature in others. Art has a remarkable ability to get through to people on topics they otherwise would not engage with. If you are willing to do so, share your river project widely and let your enthusiasm catch on. In general, people love to hear about an interesting art project that is a bit out of the ordinary, and many people have an unexpressed love for their local river. Don't underestimate the potential impacts of sharing your work online, on social media, or writing or speaking about the how nature has positively affected your life.

Be the Eyes on the Ground

Even if you are not the type of person who likes to share their work or you don't have time or money to spare, you can still make a difference by continuing to observe your river as often as you can. The simplest way that we can give back to nature is to love and care for it in our daily lives. Pollution incidents, litter, and other hazards often go unspotted, so if you can be the eyes on the ground and report anything you notice, this is a valuable contribution.

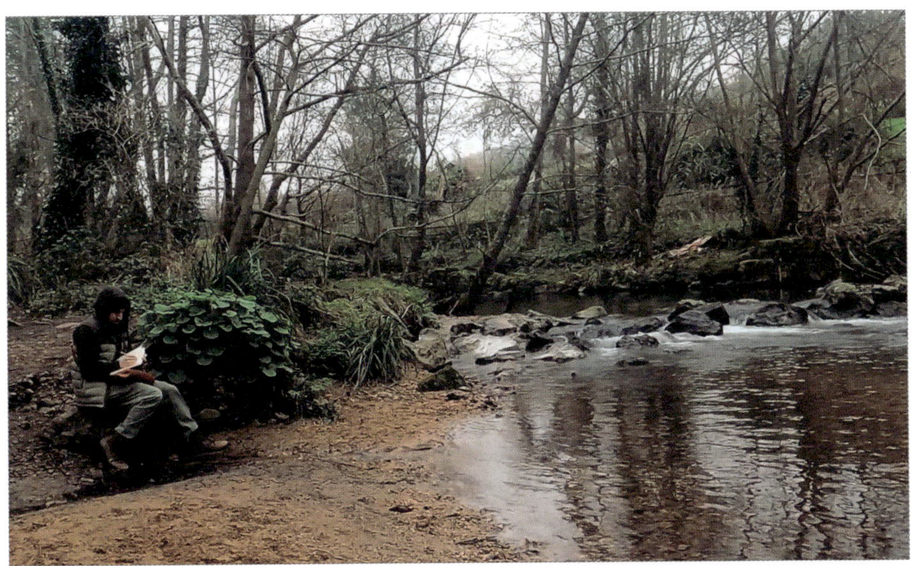

Community Effort

A few years ago, one of the tributaries of my local river was damaged by a major pollution incident. Watching the recovery of the river, and the uptake of monitoring and recording by local volunteers, has been a source of comfort and hope. Despite the damage done, the community was moved to help, and gradually nature has recovered.

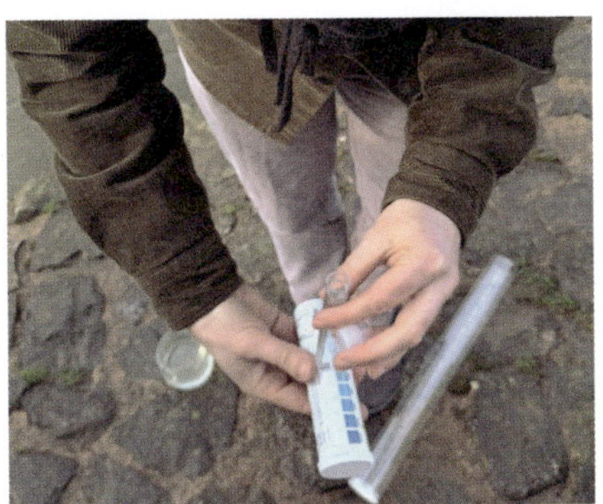

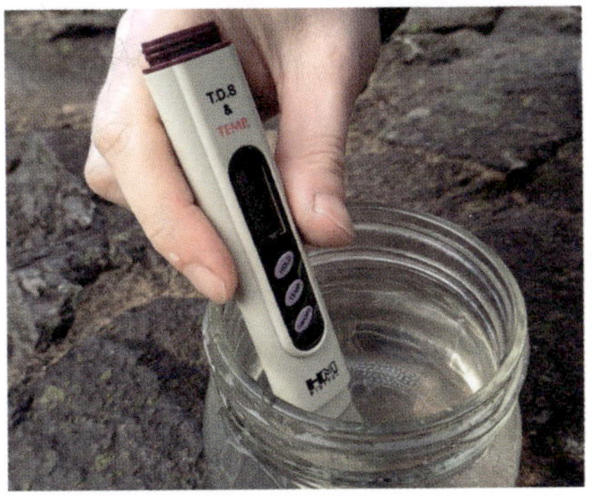

Your creation of a river log or sketchbook is part of an important movement of artists noticing and documenting the changes to the natural world. Thank you for noticing and recording, whether you share or not.

Resources

Nature Journaling

The Wild Wonder Foundation – An excellent resource for nature journalers and nature journaling teachers worldwide. www.wildwonder.org

International Nature Journaling Week – This week-long, international initiative runs every year in the first week of June. www.naturejournalingweek.com

Journaling with Nature – This excellent website and podcast features nature journals from all around the world. www.journalingwithnature.com

Identification Apps

Pay attention to an app's certainty ratings. These platforms run on artificial intelligence and are not always correct!

iNaturalist and iNaturalist Seek (International) – These great apps allow you to join a community of enthusiastic recorders of nature.

Merlin (International) – Imagine you could find out which bird is singing as you stand outside in nature... you can with this amazing app.

ObsIdentify (UK and Europe) – An excellent app for all manner of wildlife and plant identification.

Google Lens (International) – Designed to identify all sorts of different things, not just wildlife, but can be useful in a pinch!

River Organisations

These are just a few of the hundreds of amazing river-focused organisations around the world. Seek out further international, national, or local organisations to support.

The Rivers Trust – www.theriverstrust.org

American Rivers – www.americanrivers.org

Australian River Restoration Centre – www.arrc.au

International Rivers – www.internationalrivers.org

Royalty-Free Reference Photos

It can be very helpful to have access to additional photos to support your artistic development, although I recommend that these are only used as a supplementary resource (in addition to your own photos and explorations) rather than your only source of inspiration!

Pixabay – www.pixabay.com

Pexels – www.pexels.com

You can find all the reference photographs used in the lessons here: www.flickr.com/photos/alexboonart/

Downloadable phenology wheel templates can be purchased at www.alexboonart.com/shop/

Bibliography

Writing Inspired by Rivers

Beer, Amy-Jane, *The Flow* (London, 2023)

Deakin, Roger, *Waterlog* (London, 2000)

Gunn, Neil M., *Highland River* (London, 2018)

MacFarlane, Robert, *Is a River Alive?* (London, 2025)

Nature Journaling and Art Skills

Blockley, Ann, *Poetic Woods* (London, 2023)

Foxon, Ali, *The Green Sketching Handbook* (London, 2022)

Hollender, Wendy, *Botanical Drawing in Color* (New York, 2010)

Laws, John Muir, *The Laws Guide to Nature Drawing and Journaling* (Berkeley, 2016)

Walker Leslie, Claire, *Keeping a Nature Journal* (New York, 2021)

Further Inspiration

There are hundreds of illustrated nature books on my shelves – in fact, collecting older, often out-of-print, editions of nature journals and naturalist's sketchbooks is a bit of a hobby of mine! There are many, many books I could mention, but here are just a few of my absolute favourites that have greatly influenced my work and that I hope will inspire you too.

Baty, Patrick, *Nature's Palette* (London, 2021)

Bilclough, Annemarie (Ed.), *Beatrix Potter: Drawn to Nature* (London, 2021)

Brown, Jo, *Secrets of a Devon Wood* (London, 2020)

Hockney, David and Gayford, Martin, *Spring Cannot Be Cancelled* (Stoke-on-Trent, 2022)

Hoffman, Mary Jo, *Still: The Art of Noticing* (New York, 2024)

Holden, Edith, *The Country Diary of an Edwardian Lady* (London, 1977)

MacFarlane, Robert and Morris, Jackie, *The Lost Words* (London, 2017)

Oliver, Mary, *A Thousand Mornings* (London, 2018)

About the Author

Alex Boon is an artist and nature journaling educator. He studied environmental science to PhD level before deciding to leave academia and move to the countryside. He spends his days wandering the wild places, documenting nature in words and sketches, and sharing what he finds on YouTube, Instagram, and with his Nature Journaling Circle community. His greatest joy is inspiring other people to get into nature and helping them to explore their creativity. His biggest inspirations are Edith Holden, Beatrix Potter, Flora Thompson, and Jackie Morris. When he isn't drawing or exploring nature, he enjoys playing piano and doing ashtanga yoga. He lives by the sea with his partner Davey and their beloved cat, Luna.

For more about Alex visit www.alexboonart.com or follow @alexboonart on Instagram and YouTube.

Acknowledgements

As a first-time author-illustrator, I greatly appreciate the opportunity given by Nigel Browning and the team at David & Charles to produce not just one but two nature art books! Thank you to Katie Hardwicke for helping to smooth out the text and to the design team for turning a portfolio loaded with drawings into the book you hold in your hands. I would like to thank Devon Artist Network for providing me with the encouragement of a bursary award and a session with the excellent photographer Jim Wileman, whose beautiful photos have been included in this book. Thanks are also due to Davey Atkinson, Anna Brewster, and Steve Boon for support through the process of creating these books, and all the Nature Journaling Circle community members for believing in me and helping to build an online space for mindful outdoor creativity.

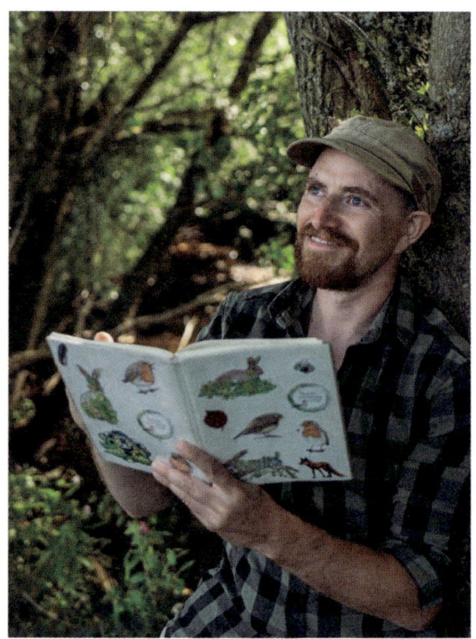

Index

A DAVID AND CHARLES BOOK

David and Charles is an imprint of David and Charles, Ltd, Suite A, Tourism House, Pynes Hill, Exeter, EX2 5WS

First published in the UK and USA in 2025

A catalogue record for this book is available from the British Library.

ISBN-13: 9781446314807 hardback
ISBN-13: 9781446314852 EPUB

This book has been printed on paper from approved suppliers and made from pulp from sustainable sources.

Printed in China by Asia Pacific Offset for:
David and Charles, Ltd, Suite A, Tourism House, Pynes Hill, Exeter, EX2 5WS

10 9 8 7 6 5 4 3 2 1

Publishing Director: Ame Verso
Commissioning Editor: Nigel Browning
Publishing Manager: Jeni Chown
Editor: Jessica Cropper
Project Editor: Katie Hardwicke
Lead Designer: Sam Staddon
Designers: Nikki Ellis & Jess Pearson
Pre-press Designer: Susan Reansbury
Illustrations: Alex Boon
Photography: Alex Boon
Anna Brewster (page 7)
Jim Wileman (page 126)
Production Manager: Beverley Richardson

David and Charles publishes high-quality books on a wide range of subjects. For more information visit www.davidandcharles.com.

Share your art with us on social media using #dandcbooks and follow us on Facebook and Instagram by searching for @dandcbooks.

Layout of the digital edition of this book may vary depending on reader hardware and display settings.